Journal of an Officer in the King's German Legion

Journal of an Officer in the King's German Legion

Recollections of Campaigning During the Napoleonic Wars

John Frederick Hering

Journal of an Officer in the King's German Legion:
Recollections of Campaigning During
the Napoleonic Wars
by John Frederick Hering

First published under the title
Journal of an Officer in the King's German Legion

Leonaur is an imprint
of Oakpast Ltd

ISBN: 978-1-84677-640-3 (hardcover)
ISBN: 978-1-84677-639-7 (softcover)

http://www.leonaur.com

Publisher's Notes

In the interests of authenticity, the spellings, grammar and place names used have been retained from the original editions.

The opinions of the authors represent a view of events in which he was a participant related from his own perspective, as such the text is relevant as an historical document.

The views expressed in this book are not necessarily those of the publisher.

Contents

Preface

The editor of the following work conceives that it possesses three separate sources of interest;—the authenticity of the narrative; the importance of the scenes wherein the journalist was engaged; and their singular variety;—to these advantages, it is scarcely too much to add, a pleasant *naiveté* of style and of remark, particularly on the author's first visit to this country, when his mind was,, of course, excited, and his attention fixed, by the striking novelty of the manners and customs whereby he was surrounded. But his story, like a moving panorama, is constantly making way; and thus, even were his "observations on men and things" oppressed with dullness, like Sinbad with the Old Man of the Sea, the "gentle reader" has little opportunity given of voting him a bore.

In addition, it may be necessary to state, for the clear understanding of some portions of the work, that the Author was attached to the medical staff of the German Legion, a circumstance which enabled him to take a more comprehensive view of the scenes acting around him.

The following is the Author's own account of his motives in writing his *Journal*.

> When the period had arrived at which I was enabled to carry into execution my purpose of entering military service in the King of England's German Legion, I gave a promise to one of my relations that I would forward intelligence to him, from time to time, of everything interesting which might occur to me personally, and of whatever

I might find around me worthy of remark.

This promise, so far as time and circumstances would allow, I faithfully kept; and, consequently, on returning to Germany, I found that a regular memoir of my twelve years' service had been thus collected.

Hence it will appear that this *Journal* was not originally destined to undergo public scrutiny, but merely designed for the amusement and information of my private circle; and although, from the time of its completion, I have received the strongest encouragement to commit it to the press, yet I have suffered ten years to intervene, in the idea that, probably, some more accomplished pen might be exercised in erecting a literary monument to the honour of that distinguished corps, in which I was proud to be enrolled, and which, in foreign lands and at an epoch pregnant with fate, upheld so courageously and happily the military fame of my native Hanover.

But since, to the general surprise, no work of this kind has hitherto appeared, I have again taken up my own *Narrative*, which I now present to the public, pretty much in the same state as when, often amidst the very uproar of battle, it issued from my pen.

I beg to be understood as not proposing to give a regular history of the German Legion; and far less a complete, scientific, military work. The title of the book itself, in fact, sufficiently explains its nature; and I have only further to observe that, in its composition, neither the wish to shine as an author, nor the consideration of pecuniary benefit, has predominated.

Introductory Account of the Formation of the German Legion

As, since the first embodying of this corps (styled, in the official acts, the "King's German Legion") upwards of twenty years have now elapsed, it may not be uninteresting to many, in the absence of a more circumstantial history, to be furnished, at any rate, with some account, however incomplete, of its rise, progress, and disbandment. I shall refrain here from making more than a bare allusion to those painful events which originally gave birth to this corps—the rather as their harassing effects may be in some measure traced in the opening of my narrative.

The idea was undoubtedly a happy one:—for, in the first place, it ensured to the officers and soldiers of the existing Hanoverian army means of carrying on their profession in an honourable manner; and secondly, opportunity was hereby given to the brave and spirited youth of that kingdom to enlist their exertions in the common European cause, and thus assist in working out eventually the redemption of their native country. A noble purpose, and nobly was it sustained!

The formation of the King's German Legion took place in the summer of 1803. In that year, the Emperor Napoleon, (then First Consul,) slighting the consideration that Hanover had one common Prince with England, despatched a French army to the frontiers of the land, and sent instructions to its General (Mortier, afterwards Duke of Treviso,) in a style so laconic as to be almost ludicrous.[1] Out of these measures sprang

1. *"Je vous ordonne de conquerir le Pays d'Hanovre!"*

the Convention of Sulingen[2] between the Hanoverian Deputies and General Mortier, the chief article whereof provided that the Hanoverian troops were to fell back behind the Elbe, and not to serve against France until they should be exchanged for French soldiers imprisoned in England.

His Britannic Majesty, however, declined ratifying this Convention, under the plea that the enemy's possession of Hanover was not justified by the laws of war. In consequence of this refusal, a capitulation was entered into between Mortier and the general-in chief of the Hanoverian forces, (Field-Marshal Von Wallmoden-Gimbors,) by virtue whereof the Hanoverian army was broken up and dismissed, with passports for their respective homes, for one year.

The Duke of Cambridge had returned to England before the entry of the French troops, and shortly after the capitulation most of our officers followed him. The attachment of the Royal Family towards their old hereditary dominions probably instigated, in the first place, the formation of a regiment of Hanoverians:—to the Duke of Cambridge was committed the carrying this idea into execution; and it is but fair to award his Royal Highness the greatest praise for his conduct in the business.

But no sooner was the new standard raised than my fellow-countrymen flocked around it in such numbers as to occasion (in the autumn of the same year) the extension of the proposed regiment into a Royal German Legion, the Duke of Cambridge being appointed colonel-in-chief thereof, as well as colonel of the First Battalion of the line. Trustworthy agents, both military and civil, were empowered to recruit privately, in Hanover, as also in the adjacent countries. They procured passports for such men as enlisted, and provided for their maintenance as far as the coast,[3] when they were received on ship-board, and treated as

2. On the 3rd of June, 1803.

3. The usual points of embarkation were Husum, Tönningen, and at the mouth of the Weser.

4. They were engaged for seven years, or until six months after the signing of peace.

soldiers.[4] The officers had to defray the expenses of their passage, and on their arrival in England received an allowance, until placed on service.

At the commencement the Legion was weak; but in September, 1805, when the war with Austria drew the French troops from Hanover, it departed, such as it then was, for Germany, under the command of General Don, who called the Hanoverians to arms; and within three months, the corps had increased to nearly 10,000 men, who, after the unhappy termination of hostilities, re-embarked for England in the January of the following year. The officers were nearly all Hanoverians; but the privates, (allowing for those removed by death or inability to serve, whose places were again filled up,) at length, consisted one half of the natives of various German states.

The military spirit and fame in arms of the old Hanoverians were, if possible, raised to a still higher pitch of glory by this Legion in many battles, sieges, and expeditions in Germany, Ireland, Sweden, Denmark, Portugal, Gibraltar, Spain, Italy, Sicily, Brabant, Flanders, Malta, and France. It was at Salamanca that its brilliant services obtained for the officers permanent rank in the English army, as was subsequently confirmed by Act of Parliament, in 1812.

After the first Paris peace, many of the veterans were dismissed; but on Napoleon's return from Elba, they were again called to service. The part which the Legion bore in the battle of Waterloo—so happy an event for the whole world—is yet fresh in the memory of every military man, and is of a character never to be forgotten.

The final dissolution of the corps in the year 1816, was effected by its being incorporated into the Hanoverian army. Such warriors as were still serviceable, and desirous of pursuing their calling, were immediately grafted into these ranks. Those who preferred returning to their homes were allowed three pence a mile (if not wounded) for travelling expenses thither. The wounded, or such as had become unfit for service, received appropriate pensions, according to the degree of their mutilation or other suffering in the service. The officers were put upon half-pay, and each disabled officer had a pension assigned him according to his rank, and which was continued to his wife, and children. In this truly paternal way did his Majesty and the noble English nation show their care of and respect for a corps, so distinguished by its martial achievements.

It may here be remarked that, during the time the enemy was in possession of Hanover, a so-styled French German Legion was formed, which, as far as I can understand, consisted of a pretty numerous body of men, and served principally in Italy and Spain, distinguishing itself particularly before Gaeta. It was chiefly composed of individuals collected from the Hanse Towns; and, I believe, had few Hanoverians in its ranks, and no officer of that nation.

Chapter 1

Departure From Home

It was in the early part of August, 1804, that the course of events which then agitated Europe summoned the flower of the youth of Hanover, my native country, across the ocean, to rally around the throne of their sovereign.

I was obliged, among the rest, to relinquish my dear Minden, the Tempe of Germany, to breathe in England a freer political atmosphere, and to work out for the future a more desirable state of things than I could anticipate from the clouded condition of my native land. The severe restrictions laid by the French upon freedom of action rendered it necessary for me to conceal my purpose, which, indeed, I could scarcely venture to disclose even to my nearest connexions and tried friends, from the fear of incurring, somehow or other, if not actual prevention or imprisonment, at least temporary hindrance.

Many of my acquaintances, it is true, despite the excess of my precaution, guessed at the motive which actuated me in leaving Minden; but, under our unfortunate circumstances, they could not but pardon my apparent want of confidence. Such a departure, it may readily be inferred, was, in its reserve and secrecy, doubly sorrowful. Those whom I left behind were near and dear to me; and whether I should ever again behold them, or under what auspices, were questions wrapt in the impenetrable gloom of the future, more particularly as I was about to tempt my fate in a foreign land.

I was accompanied by a friend to Göttingen, which town,

also, contained friends,—a separation from whom was still more painful than from those at Minden; for here I had to bid farewell to my mother and family. After I had undergone this scene, I threw myself hastily into the diligence, and proceeded towards my ulterior destination.

My fellow-passengers were quite various in their appearance;—consisting of a gay young tradesman, a melancholy widow, and a country-schoolmaster, with his wife and child, the latter of whom was perpetually screaming, This medley, combined with the jolting of the abominable carriage, (at that period constructed far more disagreeably than now!) did not a little increase the comfortless tone of my mind, already nicked with painful images, although it gave to those images another direction. I therefore, after awhile forced my thoughts into a prospective course, seeking, in contemplation of the future, an escape from the misery of the immediate past and the present.

We arrived, about the middle of a very hot day, at Nordheim, where, as it was the first point at which I encountered French, troops, I had to dread a strict examination of my passport My alarm was needless, however, as yet; and, owing to a long delay at the coach-office, I was enabled to call on a few intimate friends, to whom I communicated the secret of my expedition. At length we started again, and crawled on to Einbeck, where we arrived at sunset, having thus expended a whole day in making a journey of about twenty miles,—a distance, now accomplished in half the time.

Whilst we were changing horses the following night at Brüggen, a Frenchman came running up, and began abusing the *conducteur* for not having waited for him, through which negligence, he said, he had been obliged to travel all the distance from Einbeck on foot, although it was agreed between him and the proprietor of the vehicle, that it should stop for him at a certain spot. The *conducteur* excused himself, on the plea of ignorance as to this arrangement; and we all made merry with the idea, that this arrogant foreigner had not succeeded in putting us to inconvenience for his, perhaps, whimsical accommodation.

After a tedious journey, we at length entered, with joyous feelings, the gates of Hanover. Here I found a point of rest, although for a brief time—the diligence not going further until after the lapse of twelve hours, by which means I gained time to procure certain letters of recommendation, necessary to my appointment in the King's German Legion,—a matter wherein the good offices of my brother, who resided here, proved highly serviceable. Late in the evening I quitted the capital in a sufficiently mournful mood, which was aggravated by the gathering dust and the oppressive sultriness of the atmosphere, announcing a storm.

Midnight had passed before the insufferable heat relaxed; but, about that period, the friendly stars rushed forth, and a fresh, beautiful morning ushered us into Celle. My fellow-passengers had been gradually dropped at different points of the road; and thus my thoughts were left in freer liberty to recur to the sad circumstances attending my departure from home. Yet it frequently happens upon a journey, that too sooner has one fairly started than a multitude of little occurrences takes place which tend effectually to divert the channel of one's ideas,—and, in the present instance, such were not wanting; for, towards midday, one of Job's comforters arrived, bringing news that the conveyance which was following with our luggage had upset, and that several trunks, &c. were either missing or fairly soaked through with wet; and, to mend matters as far as regarded myself, it subsequently appeared that I was the greatest, if not the only, sufferer.

This intelligence was the more embarrassing, since one of my trunks contained, besides cash, certain papers which, in case of discovery, would involve not only myself but others, in considerable difficulties,—the slightest connexion with England being then visited as a crime. I could not accurately learn the fate of this trunk; and my only resource was, to confide in the post-master, whom it was fair to presume was no admirer of the French, and, consequently, not inclined to play me fake. I was not deceived; for this honest man pledged himself, in the most hearty manner, to spare no trouble in endeavouring to repossess me of my lost treasure, and forward it to an appointed address in Haarburg.

Nothing, however, is more tormenting than a state of uncertainty; and the desert heath across which we now journeyed, together with a Jewess who happened to sit next me, and, contrary to the habits of her caste, preserved perfect silence, did not serve to alleviate my chagrin. I, therefore, tried a change of position, and settled myself next a smart-looking young female, whom I hoped would compensate, by her volubility, for the reserve of my former neighbour: but alas! I reckoned without my host; for this fair lady, having just lost her spouse, entertained me with lucubrations more fitted for the kingdom of the dead! In this hopeless condition, I was delighted to arrive, at midday, at Haarburg.

According to my agreement with the post-master, I was obliged to remain here, and await the arrival of my trunk, which delayed me four tedious days; whilst, to render my situation more agreeable, this frontier-town was completely thronged with French military who kept a suspicious eye upon all travellers, a circumstance which compelled me to limit my daily promenades about the town and harbour.

One day, an excursion of this kind led me to the Black Mountain, as it is called, and I found a battalion of the enemy's troops exercising there, to which I felt no inclination to approach particularly near. But the exquisite prospect which this hill commands, including the city of Hamburgh, with its six lofty and gilded towers, and the city of Altona close by it;—the town of Lüneburg to the right; and, to the left, Stade, half developed and half retiring from view, was sufficient to quiet my perturbation, and smooth my indignant brow for several hours after.

The day following, to my great satisfaction, I perceived, whilst still some way off the object of my anxiety safely stowed at top of the advancing diligence, and had now nothing further to do in Haarburg but get my trunk to the inn, settle my account, hurry towards, the vessel which was to convey me to Hamburgh, and thus escape, as quickly as possible, from the French inquisition with which the inhabitants of the place were nightly visited.

No sooner had I got on board, (where several other passengers were assembled,) than a post arrived in the town which had been kept back a day owing to the French blockade of Bremen; this circumstance occasioned a delay in our sailing, whereby the *gen d'arme* gained an opportunity of examining more scrupulously our several passports. With many he expressed himself dissatisfied; and hence my fears were aroused as to the fate of my own, though I had every reason to believe it correct; so that, when he at last fell to scrutinizing it, and was in the act of comparing the personal description, my heart began to palpitate a little, and with no small delight did I receive the document back, unaccompanied by any observation. I was now happy again; and the more so, as, in that very moment, the vessel got under weigh.

Although the wind was not the most favourable, yet in three hours we found ourselves alongside the Baumhause, of Hamburgh. The passage, however, was rendered unpleasant by a heavy side wind, which threw the vessel upon her beam-ends, and thoroughly unsettled the passengers; indeed, at times, when the sails were not shortened with sufficient promptitude, it appeared as if the ship would actually upset.

How glad, nay, how happy did I now feel myself at the consciousness that I had secured my liberty, and that I ran no further risk of being deterred from prosecuting my voyage. I lost no time in ascertaining the period of the coach's departure for Husum, which, however, it appeared, would not take place for some days, and thus I had time enough to get a view of the most remarkable objects in this celebrated mart of commerce. The forest of masts by which Hamburgh had been usually distinguished had now, owing to the vicissitudes and tempests of war, completely vanished; its quays no longer exhibited a mass of busy labourers, and hence the place wore the air of desertion, silence reigning in those haunts which had formerly been crowded with merchants and mariners.

At the Altona gate I observed several hundred persons who

had, in former times, perhaps, gained a livelihood by the loading or unloading different vessels, employed in razing the city walls, and filling up the moats. Nothing could more strongly illustrate the change of time and circumstances than witnessing the demolition of these formidable barriers!

The days had passed wherein the brave citizens were enabled to defend themselves against foreign assault by help of their municipal bulwarks, in lieu of which a small force, scarcely sufficient for defence, was now substituted. Walls and ramparts could no longer preserve them! They were already threatened by the approach of the enemy; and, in short, Hamburgh presented, at that time, no single point upon which the eye could rest with pleasure. How speedily, thank God! has a revolution of events again taken place.

After I had received a fresh passport from the Danish ambassador, I travelled on by way of Altona, but found, to my cost, that the Holstein diligences were far from accommodating. They consisted, at that period, of open carriages shaped not unlike baskets, each of which was drawn by three horses abreast, who pranced along with sufficient rapidity, but kicked and plunged diabolically; and it happened, fortunately for the passengers, that the vehicle had to pass over numerous sandy tracks. On the other hand, a very praiseworthy arrangement exists in that part of the country, namely that, at every half-post, the publicans are ready prepared with refreshments for the expected travellers. The postilions, however, at present, dare not stop at will.

We passed through Pinneberg, and, towards evening, reached Elmshorn, where the road proceeded through a large inn; but the postilions, not being in the pay of mine host, made straight on to the coach-office. Our departure from this place was gloomy enough, for night was coming on, the sky looked threatening, and I, sitting in this uncovered vehicle, was exposed to all its angry humours; in fact, after awhile, the rain descended in torrents, and I was, of course, completely drenched. By daybreak we arrived at Itzehoe, and had still five miles to travel across a most desert heath to Schobstädt, which formed the next post.

In this village we found it difficult to procure either "entertainment for man or beast," as it was merely a by-road, frequented only on account of the Elbe blockade, then in existence. The relay of horses was necessarily fetched from the plough, and the postilion, a young lad first freed from the domination of his schoolmaster. A village pastor, who entered the diligence with me, stated that he was now on his way to preach a trial-sermon, for the prize attached to which no less than thirty candidates were striving.

In the afternoon we entered the pretty little town of Haide, which, at the spacious marketplace, contains a church smaller even than either of the houses adjoining it. This town being, on account of its cross-roads, a famous rendezvous for different vehicles, I had an opportunity of getting a little rest, and it was late in the evening before the signal was given for our further progress. We now soon found ourselves in the Holstein-Marsh country, and, towards morning, were on the banks of the Eyder, which we crossed by means of a flying-bridge, the construction whereof appeared to be most firm and ingenious, and well calculated to resist the strong flood and heavy torrent of that impetuous river.

In Frederickstadt, which we speedily reached, the inhabitants, notwithstanding the morning was now advanced, all seemed, without exception, bound in the silken fetters of sleep. It was the Sabbath, and, perhaps, they imagined this to be one method of keeping it holy. Hence some delay arose in the operations necessary to enable us to pursue our journey.

The most-frequented road from Frederickstadt is that by Tönningen—the least-frequented that by Husum. My fellow-passengers agreed in taking the former, and accordingly I got a whole coach to myself, which, however, to the no small delight of the postilion, I soon shared with a blind gentleman. We continued our course along dyke-roads, between deep marsh-lands filled with the finest sheep and oxen; and still, as we passed along, I remarked that the air became more bleak and severe, which I attributed to our approaching the shore of the North Sea. From the flat nature of the country, Husum became visible long before we reached it; indeed, at times, it appeared to lie almost within a bow-shot, but the numerous windings of the road greatly increases the distance.

Upon arriving at Husum, I lost no time in transacting various little matters connected with my voyage; and, towards evening, received intelligence that, should the wind prove favourable, the packet-boat wherein I had secured a place would sail on the morrow. The wind, however, was unaccommodating, and, therefore, I had no choice but to remain on shore.

It is not easy to describe the sensations with which one regards the broad ocean for the first time. A feeling of exalted admiration is strangely mixed and mingled with an emotion of shuddering fear. The town wherein I was now awaiting a prosperous gale, although situated upon an eminence, so closely overhangs the sea that, in flood-tide, the billows dash their foam upon the very fronts of the buildings. The town is long rather than broad; and, to a stranger, the innumerable nests of storks, absolutely formed upon the house-tops, present a very curious appearance; the noise, however, of these birds, is sufficient to drive an invalid to distraction. The inhabitants of Husum wear the aspect of robust strength and health.

Chapter 2

Sea-sickness

On the morning of Tuesday, the 14th of August, the captain of the packet-boat came, about six o'clock, into my room, and awoke me, saying that I must be on board within an hour, as the wind blew favourably from the east, whereby he should be enabled immediately to set sail. I hastily dressed myself, had my luggage conveyed to the harbour, and went, meanwhile, to take leave of Capt. N——, who was staying at Husum for the purpose of forwarding to England the recruits for the German Legion, and from whom I had received many marks of kindness. He was even polite enough to accompany me to the harbour; and, on my arrival there, I saw a little boat, scarcely twelve feet in length and six in breadth, into which I was stowed, together with eleven other individuals and their moveables, so that I had enough to do to preserve my personal equilibrium, and was quite disqualified from sentimentalizing (as I might, perhaps, otherwise have done) upon the occasion of quitting, possibly forever, my maternal earth.

The wind blew fresh, and, in half an hour, we reached the packet wherein our voyage was to be made, being each obliged to pay a dollar for our passage thus far! It was certainly a high charge, but is not a solitary instance of the advantage taken, by knavish persons, of peculiar circumstances. Immediately after us arrived another of these small craft, with fifty recruits for the legion; and, subsequently, the captain himself, with a stock of fresh provisions. At first, I could not imagine how it was possible to accommodate in this vessel, infinitely smaller than I had expected to find it, so many men and so much luggage. By degrees, however, all got tolerably well stowed.

Hardly had another packet-boat, which had been lying near us, got under weigh, and our own sails been unfurled, and anchor weighed, before the wind changed to the north-west, and the heavens, which had previously been beautifully clear, became obscured by heavy clouds. Notwithstanding, as the wind was not directly contrary, we sailed on, between two rather awkward sandbanks, on account of which our vessel heeled a good deal. It soon, however, blew a gale, which had the effect of tossing our bark to that degree, that few of the passengers could keep their legs:—in fact, several of the recruits, who had been piously drinking, until they could scarcely see, to the success of their native land, stood no small chance of tumbling overboard. Having proceeded in this manner some hours, the wind veered again, and, unfortunately, still more to our disadvantage.

The flood-tide was also opposed to us, whilst the neighbouring sand-banks did not permit us to tack. In this dilemma it became necessary to cast anchor at the distance of little more than seven miles from Husum, which was still plainly in sight; and the motion of the ship having acquired a new *impetus*, we swung from one side to the other in much the same manner as if in a cradle.

Whilst lying here at anchor, the captain divided the recruits into parties of eight men each, distributing to every party a wooden dish filled with yellow *pease* and meal for dinner. I was at a loss, at first, to comprehend how, in so narrow a space, these provisions could be cooked; but soon had an opportunity of clearing my doubts by the sight of the huge saucepan, and by discovering that the English method of dressing meat is more speedy than ours, as they do not like it boiled near so much: the great beat arising from the coal-fire, likewise, expedited the process.

For the cabin-passengers, who consisted (exclusive of the captain) of a lady, an officer, and myself, it was yet too early an hour, and, accordingly, a sort of lunch was placed before us, for which the keen sea-air had given us a considerable appetite. In the afternoon the atmosphere cleared up and grew more pleasant, but the wind still continued in our teeth. The heaving of the vessel, however, gradually subsided, and at four o'clock, p.m. we were able to take our first dinner on board in tolerable comfort. In order, I suppose, that the meal might be characteristic of his country, the captain regaled us with roast beef and its usual appurtenances: and as the recruits were now considered in the light of English military, they received, towards evening, the customary allowance of bread, butter, and rum.

Although in the directions of north, south, and east, land was still visible, I had the satisfaction, for the first time, of witnessing the splendid effect of the sun setting over the ocean. Our ship, as I have already observed, was of narrow dimensions when viewed in reference to a company of seventy-four persons; and hence, particularly during night, our room was necessarily circumscribed. My crib was situated in the third range in the cabin; and being almost blocked up by chests and other impediments, and not above a yard in height, I had considerable difficulty in getting into it

On the following morning, the wind chopped about towards the south, whereby we were extricated from our vexatious retardment. Although not able to make much way by means of this side-current, yet about noon we had lost sight of land, a sensation very peculiar when experienced for the first time. But another species of sensation now attacked our raw recruits, produced by the increased motion of the packet. They grew, in fact, for the most part, dreadfully qualmish; and I soon found it necessary to go upon deck, in order to free myself from the witnessing of certain consequences, which might have been instrumental in reducing me to a similar condition.

The succeeding night we proceeded without obstruction, although slowly, and before morning I was aroused by indications of an approaching tempest. As day broke the clouds divided; and the air felt purer, and, at the same time, colder, the. farther we got out. This afternoon our pilot left us, as we had now plenty of sea-room. We should, by right, have reached Heligoland the same evening, but could not get beyond the last red tun, which mark, placed in order to point out unsafe water, is shaped like a sugar-loaf, and varies in size only from several others which we had passed. I observed, by means of my glass, a number of seals upon some adjoining sandbanks.

As evening advanced, the weather once more looked suspicious, and the storm with which we had been repeatedly threatened came on in good earnest about midnight. The lightning was vivid and incessant; the thunder broke overhead in frightful peals; whilst, to aid the uproar, the side-wind screeched and howled amongst the tackling, and the seamen answered it with loud exclamations, not always of the most delicate kind.

Nor were either the women or the recruits backward in contributing their share to the harmony; and, for my own part, I was tossed to and fro in my hammock like a ball. We shipped several very heavy seas, and the crew were anxiously employed in taking in sail: shortly after, the pumps were all in action, as the water had penetrated almost every part of the vessel. All this, being quite a novel thing to me, excited feelings of no enviable description; and, indeed, to say the truth, I was in a state of very undignified alarm.

There was, however, as it proved, no great occasion for my terror. The gale subsided with the return of day, and, to my unspeakable satisfaction, I. heard the captain announce, from the upper deck, that Heligoland was in sight, before which place it was his intention to anchor. I hastened up from below, and beheld, to my astonishment, waves running mountains high, upon whose snowy crest the island before me absolutely appeared to be dancing, whilst our little bark was hurled about like a shuttlecock, and seemed as if every instant it would be sucked in by the greedy and insatiate billows.

The cold, cutting air did not permit me to gaze long upon this curious although somewhat fearful spectacle, especially as the deck was frequently washed by the waves, and, consequently, all those individuals thoroughly drenched whom curiosity had attracted from their hammocks. About seven o'clock we cast anchor as near to Heligoland as the adjacent shoals would allow us to do, and found some shelter even from this neighbourhood to its rocky coast. The two English frigates which were blockading the passage of the Elbe likewise lay here. A few hours later, our jaded company found great satisfaction in the refreshment of coffee and its accompaniments.

We were compelled to remain here seven long days—a period which seemed inconceivably tedious, the more so as the motion of the vessel, while at anchor, is even worse than when at sea; in addition to which the chill, damp sea air struck us most inhospitably, and we were not without fears that we might be driven from our anchorage. Our provisions, also, began to grow scanty, and these unpleasant circumstances altogether, joined to the influence of the sea-sickness, which had not yet wholly quitted us, tendered our situation sufficiently irksome. By good luck, on the fifth day a packet-boat passed us from England, by whose help we were furnished with a fresh supply of biscuit, had it not been for which we should, infallibly, have found it necessary to go back to Husum.

This packet-boat anchored here for the propose of procuring a pilot; and it was with considerable difficulty our captain got on board her, in order to solicit the supply which the continued rough-state of the sea prevented our getting from Heligoland. Water, it is true, we had for four weeks in advance, but it was becoming daily less and less drinkable, owing to the violent action of the ship: our master assured us, however, meanwhile, that, in case of urgency, our wants would be relieved by the frigates formerly alluded to. The number of vessels at anchor here, in fact, had gradually increased, until, one morning, I could count seventeen.

It is a very interesting spectacle to view a ship in full sail, borne on, as is so frequently the case in these parts, by a strong current. To a beholder at some little distance, she seems as if lying completely on her side,—her keel being often distinctly visible for several minutes together. On the sixth day arrived, under convoy of a cutter, a store-ship destined for the use of the two frigates.

At length the hour of liberation approached, and it was high time! We had grown so thoroughly tired of our confinement that we had scarce spirits to go through the common duties of the day, and began to grow apprehensive that we should weary even of taking our regular meals. Indeed the personal appearance of the cook, who was miserably deficient in cleanliness, as well as the look of the eatables themselves, presented no extraordinary stimulus to the appetite.

Carelessness and listlessness had seemingly crept upon every individual, and we were enabled to estimate the misery of a becalmed state at sea. The cabin-provender consisted, generally, of roast fowls; to vary which, we had occasionally a basin of soup: it was incumbent on us, however, to indulge in these viands, particularly the latter, with caution; since it was by no means unusual for the table to make a sudden lurch, and not only upset the quietly-seated expectants, but empty into their laps the confections which had been destined for their stomachs.

On the morning of the 22nd of August, at six o'clock, the wind having changed to the north, we once more weighed anchor, and were off: we now sailed so near to the island, that the people on shore could be distinguished without difficulty. The inhabited north-western part consists of a sort of red sand-stone, and towards the eastern part the earth is soft and yielding, but influenced in a singular degree by the ebb and flood of the tide. That portion of the island which is built upon includes a space about a mile in length and one-third of a mile in breadth; but, notwithstanding, it is said that upwards of fifteen hundred persons dwell within this circumference, obtaining their living chiefly by catching fish and acting as pilots. It had, as everybody knows, its most productive season in the last war, during which it became known to many who had previously no acquaintance with the spot.

We lost sight of this naked rock in the course of an hour, and again had no object around us but sea and sky, on the former of which several vessels were dancing about at different distances. I remarked that the ocean, according as its immense surface was agitated by the wind, presented the form of mountains and valleys almost as clearly defined as those of dry land, but, unlike them, invested with never-ceasing changes. The deep green of the water, as one gets farther out, also attracts the attention of the young voyager: it is owing doubtless to the mass not being so much mixed up with land-streams more or less impregnated with earth. Whole flocks of sea-birds formed our true and constant followers; and when tired of continuing on the wing, they did not hesitate to skim upon the very surface of the highest billows.

We pursued our voyage for two days and two nights without any accident worthy notice; and on the 24th in the afternoon, the captain announced from the mast-head that land was in sight,—information which operated upon us all like magic. Even our invalids, as if by miracle, sprang up from their sick couches, and those whom the protracted passage had rendered splenetic, recovered their good-humour with equally surprising celerity.

On the succeeding morning we encountered numerous ships, and the air appeared to grow much milder as we gradually neared the coast of Suffolk. Towards midday we could discern objects upon land, such as towers and trees; and in the evening sundry lighthouses displayed themselves.

I now lay down with the agreeable anticipation that it was for the last time on board this tiresome packet-boat; nor did my presentiment turnout to be unfounded; for, upon waking in the morning, the long-wished-for intelligence was communicated that we were actually lying at anchor at the mouth of the Thames. I hurried immediately upon deck, and shall never forget the delightful sensations I at that moment experienced.

Chapter 3
Arrival in England

The morning was most serene, and the sun, gradually ascending from the depths of ocean, gilded the houses of the town of Wakering, which lies upon the left bank of the Thames, and contains a sea-bathing establishment upon rather a large scale. The wind, however, uprose with the sun; and chopping right into our teeth, combined with the ebb-tide in keeping us for a while stationary.

On the Nore, to the left of us, were lying numerous ships of war of various sizes, and the shore was completely lined with batteries. Advantage was taken of the ebb-tide by a prodigious number of coal-vessels, which were dropping down the river towards their several destinations in the provinces. Altogether, a principle of busy life was apparent, calculated to arouse even the unconcerned spectator to increased energy and spirit.

On the setting-in of the flood, we got under weigh again and sailed up the river, being still obliged (the wind remaining contrary) to tack a good deal. Hence, we often ran close along-shore; and passing in succession several pretty towns, arrived in the vicinity of Gravesend, where lay six frigates, to cover the passage. In comparison with these, our little packet cut but a sorry figure,—its masts dwindling, as it were, into walking-sticks, whilst theirs were decorated with various colours, and the order and cleanliness which appeared to prevail could not but strike a foreigner with amazement.

At the return of ebb-tide, we were once more compelled to

cast anchor, and our master went ashore to announce his arrival and make preparations for our disembarkation. He brought back with him some fresh bread; milk, cheese, &c. which, after our living so long upon sea-biscuit, were real comforts.

The ensuing flood carried us up as far as Dartford, and we could now distinguish the grand Arsenal at Woolwich and the cupola of St: Paul's, and finally, in the neighbourhood of the celebrated Greenwich Hospital, cast anchor for the last time.

On that same evening, (namely, the 26th of August,) we went ashore, and thus ended my first voyage,—the discomfort attending the early part of which was amply remunerated by the interest and pleasure of the two or three last days.

A custom-house officer superintended the disembarkation; but, so lax was his scrutiny, that I might easily have smuggled on land many contraband articles, had I been inclined to mark my first steps on the hospitable British shore by an illegal and unjust action. The case, however, is very different at the Custom-House in London, whither all the trunks and packages were conveyed in the vessel. The examination here is most strict, and cannot be eluded; and, upon a foreigner, it falls with peculiar severity.

But how singular was the sensation which I experienced on setting my foot once more upon land! Heaven and earth seemed to be all in motion,—whilst my head reeled in harmony, and my rebellious heels threatened every moment to trip me. Nevertheless, I staggered along, until I found myself upon a by-road leading from Greenwich to London. I had, at first, intended to make this little journey on foot, but the advice of a friend, added to the unsteady condition of my legs, led me to avail myself of a passing coach, whereupon imagination had sufficiently tortured itself with these gloomy ideas, I was agreeably surprised by the entrance of a well-dressed person and fellow-countryman, who told me he had been requested by the mistress of the house to come and assist in procuring me any comfort I might stand in need of.

By this timely aid, I soon found my terrors vanish and my conveniences increase. Having passed a sufficiently disagreeable night, I arose at a very early hour, but discovered that, according to English domestic habits, this would never do, for nothing was going forward in the house but scouring and cleaning, so that I scarcely found a place to sit down in.

This morning I took my first journey—for so I may fairly call it—in London, in company with my beforementioned German friend. I had to go to the Custom-house, in order to get my things examined, in doing, which, without reckoning the delay at that place itself, several hours were expended. Our road led us through St. James's Park, which is of considerable extent, but possesses no feature either of elegance or grandeur. Its principal ornaments consist of two or three straight rows of trees, an enclosed grass-plot, and a dirty pond. A few scattered benches proclaim it to be a public promenade, which is, at fifties lively enough. Of the various buildings which dirt this celebrated lounge, many are more distinguished by the purposes to which they are devoted than by an imposing exterior; and others are altogether wretched and uninteresting,

I visited, in turn, Westminster Abbey and Bridge; and, in the former venerable structure, look great pleasure in examining the royal tombs which are erected in the chapel of King Henry the Seventh. Passing from hence along the crowded Strand, one of the greatest thoroughfares in London, and full of shops wherein is piled every variety of traffic, we shot through the gloomy arch of Temple Bar, and, ascending Ludgate Hill, stood before the magnificent cathedral of St. Paul's. This huge church, the building of which occupied just a century less than that of St. Peter's, namely, thirty-five years, is composed of a peculiar species of stone, extracted from the quarries of Portland Isle. The immense dome produces an effect superior to anything of the, kind I ever before witnessed.

It is matter of deep regret that this fine structure, the greatest architectural ornament of the British capital, should be hidden by the numerous insignificant-looking houses wherewith it is closely surrounded. In fact, though situated upon an eminence, there is no getting any point of view by which its proportions can be folly seen and estimated. The interior has little decoration: no great painter has lent his aid to render illustrious the walls or altars; nor has the exercise of the sister-art of sculpture been by any means lavished upon its ornaments. With a laudable spirit of consistency, the interior circumference of the dome is decorated with flags captured by the English in their several engagements; the trophies of war being thus introduced to compose and harmonise the spirits of those who enter the temple of peace.

It is curious enough to observe that, amidst all the vast press of people and throng of carriages perpetually passing to and fro in the streets of London, very seldom does any accident whatever occur; in fact, I soon became convinced (although at first scarcely inclined to credit the thing) that nobody can possibly walk about in greater safety than here: the foot-passengers, with a kind of natural tact, make way for one another, as they proceed along the broad, beautiful pavement, which is kept in admirable order.[1] The wall is invariably given to the women; and there is no fear, if moderate caution is used, of being run down by the pole of a carriage.

We, at length, reached the Custom House, a very large edifice, at which multitudes of bales are continually received and issuing forth. I now learnt the disagreeable intelligence that my trunks, &c. had not yet been unshipped, but would, probably, be so the next day. Stress of business was alleged as the cause of this, against which it would, of course, be idle to remonstrate. There was nothing to do but to submit; and, accordingly, I again turned my face homewards. When, on the following morning, I returned, I was compelled to seek out my chests and other luggage from a regular mountain of litter. Everything was separately examined, and a small box, containing German books and instruments, reserved for further scrutiny—for which box I had eventually to pay a duty little short of two pounds!

1. The Author seems to be in a very complimentary mood just here: his praise of the good order in which the pavements are kept only citizen to remind a "Citizen" of the melancholy reverse.—Editor.

Amongst other public buildings, my attention was particularly directed to the Mansion-house, a structure which might, for extent and ornamental style, be denominated a palace: its architecture, however, although grand, is heavy; the columns appear, at the first glance, too high to harmonise with the general plan; and the interior may be termed rather splendid than tasteful.

But what most surprised and delighted me was a visit which I paid to the London Docks, one of the great receptacles for merchant-ships. A space has been cleared for this vast national work, upon which from 400 to 500 houses originally stood. The number of warehouses which line these docks is immense.

It frequently happened, during my peregrinations through the metropolis, that I heard the alarm of "fire!" and, occasionally, actually witnessed the conflagration. But it is odd enough that this kind of thing attracts little or no notice amongst the good citizens. Each man plods heedlessly forward, haying, perhaps, just turned his head aside to observe the passing of the rattling engine; and even those who live in the unlucky neighbourhood gaze listlessly from their doors or windows, viewing the scene with perfect nonchalance, until it approaches inconveniently near to their own abodes.

I one day saw an apothecary's shop in flames, the sulphurous smoke emitted from which was particularly unpleasant, and rendered everyone around desirous of escaping as quickly as possible from so noxious an effluvium. Few of the assembled worthies expressed any pity for the sufferers upon this occasion but seemed annoyed, beyond measure, by the disagreeable stench.

It happened that, on the day alluded to, I dined in company with a German gentleman, whose history possesses so much variety, that I will not scruple to lay a brief abstract of it before the reader.

Born in Brunswick, he received his education in Holstein; by dint of some manoeuvring on the part of others, he found himself entrapped into the Austrian military service, and was taken prisoner by the French in the battle on the bridge of Lodi. When upon his passage to France, on board ship, he was freed by means of the English fleet sailing to Egypt, with which the enemy's vessel had the ill luck to fall in; he now entered the British service, in which he made the campaign in Egypt, and returned, after the peace, of Amiens, to London, where he received certain prize-money, wherewith, hc commenced business, and, at the time I met him, was considered an opulent man.

The practitioners of the art of begging in London resort, occasionally, to very ingenious modes of attracting notice, of which the following exhibits, I think, a curious instance. I one day saw a fellow employed in executing sundry very elaborate pieces of painting, with chalks of different colours, upon the stones of the pavement, three or four of which he had carefully cleansed for the purpose. He professed to have been a soldier, and his subjects consisted of scenes from the various battles wherein he had been engaged, each of which had a written explanation underneath; the whole was so dexterously managed, that it was impossible to refuse the poor devil your pence and praise.

There is so strong a jealousy existing on the part of the public, in England, with regard to military men, that an officer, even if high in command, seldom wears his uniform unless actually on duty; and, indeed, often makes his servant bring his private dress to the guard-house, to avoid walking through the streets home *en militaire.* Since the successful campaigns of the Duke of Wellington, however, this characteristic prejudice has somewhat relaxed. The entire number of soldiers, actually on guard at one time in the various parts of London (the most important capital of Europe) does not, probably, exceed three hundred foot and about twenty-four horse.

Hyde Park, on a Sunday, presents a scene highly characteristic. It is flocked to, in the course of the day, by perhaps a hundred thousand people, who seem to derive infinite amusement from sauntering up and down a promenade of about a couple of miles in length, and enveloping themselves and their holiday finery in impenetrable clouds of dust.

Chapter 4

Departure From London

According to my instructions, I now began making preparations for my departure for Southampton. The coach started so early as half-past five; but as it is a custom in England never to eat before eight o'clock in the morning, I was necessitated to commence my journey with an empty stomach. The confusion and bustle which attend the setting out of an English stage-coach are almost incredible: nobody seems to understand in the least what is going on, and, in the universal disorder, I felt considerable dread lest my packages or myself should be stowed into the wrong vehicle: an alarm which (so far as I was personally concerned) subsided on perceiving that the name of the place for which each coach was destined was conspicuously inscribed upon its outside.

Both immediately before and after any stoppage, the guard blows an intolerable blast upon his still more intolerable horn—a sound which almost put me to death, more particularly as it provoked a contrast with the melodious and heart-cheering tones of the postilions of my native country. Often have I thrown myself back in a German diligence, (having bribed one of these fellows with an extra gratuity,) and listened, delightedly, to airs whose simple and touching *pathos* made all the scenes which I had quitted, with the dear human beings by whom they had been animated, come swimming into my memory!

On the stroke of six, the coach started; and already, by eight o'clock, we had changed horses twice. At about ten miles' distance from the metropolis, we arrived upon a heath several miles in extent, and upon which were scattered, here and there, little clusters of houses, differing most materially from our German huts in the cleanliness of their exterior and the neatness of their appurtenances. The disgraceful dung-heap commonly to be seen in front of a German cottage is here, at any rate, confined to the back part of the premises; and the trim glazed windows, shadowed by snug white curtains, proclaim that the fondness for comfort natural to the character of the English extends even to the humblest ranks of society.

In the afternoon, about three o'clock, we arrived at Winchester, and by six in the evening at Southampton; having thus completed seventy-five English miles in twelve hours, at the usual rate of travelling, and including stoppages which occupied two hours. At the last-mentioned place, I accidentally met with an officer by whom I was to be furnished with fresh instructions respecting my commission in the German Legion, and from him I received an appointment by virtue of which I proceeded, without delay, to join a cavalry regiment then stationed at Dorchester.

My inn at Southampton proved far more commodious than that at London. I am not, however, going to fatigue the reader by describing, in detail, my different adventures at these kind of places. Still, as I have to mark the peculiar impressions made upon me by residence in a foreign country, I may as well at once state that the larger English taverns are as decidedly inferior to those of Germany as the lesser ones are superior. Cleanliness, indeed, is quite a universal care, and seems as natural to an Englishman as the want of it does to a German, by whom it is regarded, when practised, rather as a painful duty than a pleasant refreshment. In the Southampton inn, I was a good deal surprised to find not only the rooms, but stairs also, well carpeted—a luxury scarce ever to be met with amongst us, and by which the other accommodations may be estimated.

Southampton is a pretty town, situated in a pleasant country; and the gaiety of the trading part of it almost emulates that of the metropolis. On the morning which succeeded my arrival, I journeyed on by way of Salisbury, where, having taken up my quarters at the White Hart, I made the necessary preparations to regale myself with my *meerschaum*; but, alas! hereupon arose almost as great a storm as any I had experienced at sea! My good landlady herself pounced upon me in the utmost consternation, and actually forbad the execution of my design. In this she was undoubtedly justified, smoking being generally prohibited, except in the tap-rooms of English inns. Under these desperate circumstances I sallied forth to visit the cathedral, the spire of which is said to be the loftiest in England. Its interior is adorned with a great number of magnificent Gothic columns and ancient monuments.

In the evening I pursued my route to Dorchester, which I reached next morning very early, after a disagreeable journey in a close coach, containing eight passengers, several of whom most provokingly objected to the introduction of fresh air, by means of opening the windows, even at a time when we were well nigh suffocated.

At this period there were two distinct species of barracks in England, one comprising those of a temporary, the other those of a permanent description, to which latter the Dorchester barracks appertained. They were consequently built upon a stronger and more careful construction than those which had been got up merely to suit the purpose of the moment In fact, they had ail the appearance of a little military town, and, in circumference, extended upwards of half a mile, being surrounded by a wall twelve feet high. In the centre of the upper part was situated the principal building, which was reserved for the residence of the officers.

It was a handsome-looking house, of corresponding extent and height; in front, was a neat range of columns; and the royal arms, accompanied with warlike emblems, graced a pediment above. On each wing of the officers' barracks stood a longer range, the upper rooms of which were appropriated to the non-commissioned officers and privates, whilst the ground-floor was used as stables. These three piles of building stood upon a kind of eminence, at the foot of which were two others, the one intended as the hospital for the men, the other as a receptacle for sick horses. Besides these, other structures .were included in this military station, such as a riding-house, houses for the barrack-master, &c. The whole looked very symmetrical. Nevertheless, as all our regiment could not be accommodated here, I was obliged, with other officers, to take lodgings in the town, and many of the privates were billeted in different public-houses.

On the 18th of September, being the fourth day after my arrival at barracks, I had an opportunity of beholding, for the first time, his Majesty King George the Third, who came to review our regiment, together with a train of mounted artillery, which lay at Bridport. I expected that, on this occasion, there would be an immense number of spectators assembled; but, on the contrary, I could scarcely count fifty; for, since the king made a point of visiting Weymouth every summer, to enjoy the benefit of sea-bathing, his presence was by no means novel, or calculated to produce any particular excitement.

Shortly after this occurrence, a matter of business led me to Weymouth, and I was very much struck by the beautiful prospects which exhibited themselves at different points of the journey, From an eminence upon the high road, I, at one time, could command, to the left, a large creek, wherein lay several frigates, and, amongst them, the king's yacht, whilst, on the point of land hard by, was an encampment of several thousand men.

To the right was Weymouth itself, a very pretty town: and, straight before us, as if actually springing out of the ocean, was descried the Isle of Portland. Altogether it presented one of the most imposing and cheerful *coups d'œuil* I ever beheld. The house occupied at this watering-place by the king himself was not distinguished in any way from those in the possession of the nobility and other wealthy persons.

It appeared very extraordinary to me that I should have passed six weeks in England without having witnessed a single instance of rain, notwithstanding the climate is generally esteemed so damp and watery; when at last, however, the wet weather did set in, I could not help observing the clatter of the women's pattens—a sound perfectly new to me.

The life and manners of the English farmers, of whom I had an opportunity of seeing a good deal whilst I resided in the country, exhibit great marks of cheerfulness and contentment: their sons and daughters spend their time in studying music and cultivating flower-gardens, quite heedless of the future, and desirous to emulate the ladies and gentlemen of the cities. Their mode, of existence is, however, monotonous enough, being seldom varied, except by the occasional receipt of a newspaper.

Chapter 5

Wreck of an East-Indiaman

About the middle of January our regiment changed quarters with the Heavy Dragoon Regiment of our legion, which, until then, had been stationed at Radipool. As the barracks at this place were larger than those of Dorchester, I took up my abode therein. They belonged, however, to the temporary class before alluded to, and stood hardly more than two gun-shots' distance from the sea-shore. They were of brick, and only one story high. Although it was now the middle of winter, men were employed in enlarging these barracks still more. The rooms were six feet long and proportionably broad, and were abundantly supplied with every comfort, excepting beds, by the barrack-master.

The cold weather was, by this, extreme, though it is worthy of remark that it was by no means so piercing on the beach as at some distance inland. The surge of the sea produced a most appalling noise in the stillness of evening; in fact, those who only view it in the gentle moods peculiar to the summer season can have little idea of its violence when lashed by the tempestuous gales of winter.

On the night of the 5th of February the monotony of our barrack-life was unpleasantly broken in upon by the calamitous shipwreck of an East-Indiaman on our coast, almost every soul on board perishing. The three masts of the vessel were distinctly perceptible from our station at the moment previous to her sinking. One of the crew, who had been fortunately saved, gave the following account of the particulars:—The vessel was called the *Abergavenny*, and had commenced her voyage from London to the East Indies a few days only prior to the melancholy catastrophe. Approaching too near the rocky boundary of Portland Isle, she sprang a leak, of which, however, the captain took little notice until he discovered that his ship was fast filling with water, and in danger of being lost. They now made way for land, ,as their last chance; but, owing to the contrary wind, their progress was very slow, and, with scarce any further note of preparation, down she went! Could she have got a couple of thousand paces nearer the crew might have been rescued.

This awful accident occurred at the hour of eleven, p. m.: the people on board, at the moment of the ship's sinking, endeavoured to avert their fate by clinging to the masts and rope ladders, and striving, amidst a deluge of rain, darkness, and cold, to hold on till morning. Signal-guns had been, of course, repeatedly fired by them, but the roughness of the weather prevented their being heard on shore. Exhaustion caused numbers of these poor wretches to drop, in succession, from the articles they convulsively grasped; others were washed away by the impetuous waves; and, out of a large complement of men, sixty only reached land again. Amongst others, a youth had struggled hard to save a young female, his relative, from the devouring element; no effort for this purpose was left unexerted by him,—but in vain, and they sank at last, clasped in each other's arms!

On the subsequent days, a number of persons were busily occupied in recovering portions of the valuable lading of the ship, by means of diving bells; until, at length, the billows completely dashed to pieces the sunken wreck. Bodies of the dead, by dozens, were daily washed upon the shore, and interred at the public expense.

Towards the end of February, in the southern parts of England, the cheerful Spring begins to make its appearance, and I took advantage of this to undertake several rides in the adjacent villages. Amongst these is one called Radwell, where there is a mineral spring, the water of which is said to possess peculiar virtues. Here I have frequently had the honour of meeting, attended by a single servant, the King of England, who received the water from a gentleman in a golden goblet.

The festival of Easter is observed in England, as, indeed, are all other religious festivals, as a time more peculiarly set apart for rioting and drinking. The higher orders of society, in fact, do not observe them at all; and this difference appears, at first, exceedingly strange to the continental visitor. On the Easter Monday of this year an event occurred in our neighbourhood which dashed the mirth of the populace; for, in one of these drunken revels, a dragoon met his death in an affray with a sailor.

I was one day a good deal amused by the sight of a huge fish which had been caught on the coast. Its length was thirty-six feet, and its circumference six; and it seemingly belonged to the whale genus. The colour of its skin was black, without scales; and its tail, ten feet long, was destitute of fins, but had an uncommonly thick coat: the flesh was red.

In the month of May, which, as if to illustrate the proverbial changeableness of the English climate, was prodigiously cold and stormy, the course of my service called me to St. Alban's Head. The road ran at top of the precipitous height overhanging the sea; and from hence, the largest vessels floating below us dwindled, in appearance, into minute cockboats.

Chapter 7

Royal Review

At the end of June our regiment received orders to march again to the barracks of Dorchester. The temperature had now become warm and the air genial, and the eye wandered over the rich cornfields with a feeling of great relief from the dull eternal monotony of the ocean. Our residence at the above place proved, however, to be but brief, for, in the following month, the king again visited Weymouth, to bathe; and a grand review was planned, in which we were included, and, accordingly, repaired to cantonments near that town. The situation of these was singularly agreeable, the more so on account of the beautiful season of the year.

The morning of the review having arrived, our regiment was posted upon an eminence, whereon it formed a line with the 15th English Light Dragoons. At the foot of this eminence, several trains of artillery, both English and German, were stationed. Fronting us, to the right, and close to the sea, was placed a corps of riflemen. Beyond was stretched the mighty ocean, upon which the royal yacht, with several frigates, and other vessels, were dancing to a gentle breeze. Behind us, likewise, upon a hill, a number of infantry and heavy cavalry regiments had formed themselves; and, as the whole arrangement could be overlooked readily from our post, I had an opportunity of enjoying one of the most splendid and imposing spectacles imaginable.

The king had arrived at Weymouth by six o'clock, a. m. and, at eleven, visited the body of heavy dragoons attached to our legion, which was lying at the barracks of Radipool. It was five in the afternoon, consequently, before his presence was announced in our camp; upon which circumstance being made known, the entire body of cavalry, under command of the Duke of Cumberland, passed in file before His Majesty. No sooner had the sovereign's approach from Weymouth been perceived, than he was greeted with a salute of artillery, which description of force having also been reviewed, the king rode to the body of infantry, by whom he was received with a *feu-de-joie,* three times repeated; and, no sooner was the air cleared from smoke, whilst still the music of the different regiments filled it with harmony, than the grand cannonading from the harbour began to roll its thunders through the atmosphere; the riflemen then proceeded to give their salute, which was echoed by the vessels lying off the port.

A few days after this, I saw the king and royal family return from a little cruise they had been making. The small fleet had consisted of two yachts, under convoy of a frigate, in company, besides, with two brigs and two cutters. It had sailed at nine o'clock in the morning, and returned in the evening, at six. The royal family were brought ashore in a large boat, which was steered by a naval captain, and rowed by sixteen sailors, dressed in a uniform consisting of white vests, long blue trousers, black silk neck handkerchiefs, and black caps with red feathers.

Every direction of the officer who steered was attended to with almost incredible rapidity and precision; and a salute of twenty-one cannon, together with the melody of several bands of music, signalised the disembarkation of this revered monarch, of whose command over the respect and affection of his subjects, I beheld, upon this occasion, a conspicuous instance.

Having successively had opportunities of visiting Salisbury, Northampton, Coventry, Canterbury, &c. in the course of which movements, I once or twice renewed my acquaintance with the British capital and its environs, I was apprised that, in consequence of the loss of the battle of Austerlitz, and the subsequent peace between France and Austria, all the troops in the pay of

England, that had been on the Continent, were recalled, among which my own regiment had been included, although I did not accompany it, having received an intermediate appointment in England. Upon its return, however, and disembarkation at Portsmouth, I was directed to rejoin this regiment, and, accordingly, repaired to that place.

After having remained here eight days, it was decided that we should repair to Ireland; and with this view, we had to undertake a distance of 306 miles—namely, to Liverpool. This march, however, so far from fatiguing, seemed to me almost like an excursion of pleasure, as we had to pass through, perhaps, the most beautiful part of the kingdom, at a pleasant time of year, with short stages of fifteen to twenty-five miles, and over capital roads. Our mode of living, also, was excellent, although somewhat cosily; an officer's daily expenses amounting to between nine and twelve shillings, for nothing more than ordinary meals.

From Portsmouth, we proceeded through Petersfield, Alton, and Farnham, three small towns in Hampshire; in the latter of which places we sojourned above a week, in order to afford our horses necessary respite. From hence we continued our route through Odiham and Reading; and, subsequently, along the banks of the river to Wallingford, in Berkshire. Here we were regarded with infinite curiosity; every part of our equipment which bore a foreign character being scrutinized with wondrous exactness, and even our moustaches commented on, as things of a nature almost miraculous. In fact, the English military not patronizing these warlike appurtenances, I question if the good people of Wallingford had ever witnessed a previous example.

From Wallingford, we proceeded to Oxford. Whilst still at a distance, the numerous towers and other lofty buildings of this beautiful town proclaimed it to be the seat of learning and clerical dignity. On entering it, I was particularly struck with the neatness and elegance of the whole place. The wide well-paved streets—the cleanliness everywhere apparent—and the exquisite gardens, as combined to fill me with admiration.

As one of the dignitaries of the University had the politeness to offer us admission to the most remarkable objects therein contained, we took advantage of his courtesy to inspect them.

What a great difference is apparent between the English and the German student! nor is this distinction confined to mere dress or formality, but is most perceptible in the habits and manners of the respective individuals. In our German universities, the young men are boisterous, quarrelsome, slovenly in dress, and rough in address. At Oxford, on the other hand, (and, I presume at Cambridge, also,) the students are gentlemanly in exterior, quiet,[1] and rather reserved in their demeanour; and, with their black silk cassocks and trencher-caps, present a powerful contrast to the *negligé* air, so general amongst the scholars at Tübingen or Jena.[2]

Upon leaving Oxford, we passed the observatory, which stands in an open place outside the city, on our way to Chipping-Norton, and the following day reached Shipston, where we halted.

On the 1st of April, we arrived at Birmingham, a very large and populous but ill-built town, the streets of which are narrow and without flag-stones for the foot-passengers. The manufactories in this place are numerous and extensive, but the people employed, somehow or other, can scarcely derive a bare subsistence from their utmost labour. Hence, perhaps, the stranger does not perceive here the same expenditure in dress and mode of living which strikes him in other English towns, though the principle of cleanliness still obtains. The Royal Hotel, wherein I slept, proved one of the most splendid places of public entertainment I had ever witnessed since the commencement of my expedition.

On our departure from this great manufacturing town, it is almost impossible to describe the number of gazers which the

---

1. If our author had been introduced to some of the evening revels of these very well-behaved young gentlemen, perhaps the scene might have modified his opinion, as to their quietness and reserve.

2. It is common enough to meet one of these youths attired in a shaggy great coat; immense duck trousers, meant to be taken for white; linen to correspond; and, glued to his lips, a German pipe as long as his body.

singularity of our appearance drew together, from which circumstance, is fact, our horses had no small difficulty in making their way!

By Easter we had reached the vicinity of Liverpool; but as the transport-ships, wherein a heavy dragoon regiment had been conveyed to Ireland were not yet returned, we meanwhile proceeded to St. Helen's; at which place having remained about two days, we started, early one fine April morning, for Liverpool; and, by eight o'clock, both men and horses were embarked. We had calculated on getting under weigh immediately; but the wind having veered to an unfavourable point, it became necessary for us again to disembark, (leaving the horses on board,) and to take up Our quarters in various inns—by which means I obtained an opportunity of scrutinizing more closely the superb town wherein I found myself.

The bank, the exchange, and other buildings, then unfinished, but which promised nobly, excited my particular attention, as did the variety of quays, warehouses, &c.; but the friend of humanity cannot withhold a compassionate tear when he reflects, that all this wealth and splendour owes its origin to the slave-trade!

Chapter 8

Voyage From Liverpool

We had a pleasant voyage from Liverpool, during which nothing took place worth recording; and on the fourth day after setting sail, we found ourselves in the harbour of Dublin.

The regiment having disembarked, and having been sent into barracks, the officers distributed themselves in different lodging-houses in the town, which, although I had just left Liverpool, and had resided in London, yet impressed me with ideas of magnificence superior to any I had imbibed in either of those two cities. It has broader streets than the British metropolis, and the buildings are loftier; but the evidences of opulence and business so characteristic of that matchless capital are wanting.

The hospitality of the Irish character has often been observed upon; and I am happy to add my testimony to that of the travellers who have preceded me. But there is one thing which impresses the stranger very disagreeably; I allude to the violent contrast everywhere presented between great wealth and absolute want. This is, indeed, exhibited in all possible varieties. Alongside the elegant carriage, drawn by its well-fed steeds, you frequently see the most miserable dog-cart, dragged slowly by a half-starved horse, and guided by a ragged, raw-looking native, whose meagre form and sallow face sufficiently manifest. his utter ignorance of a plentiful meal. The wretched-looking hut is often placed in curious juxtaposition with the splendid palace; and in short I might go on multiplying instances to a very inconvenient length.

Our regiment having been reviewed by the Lord-lieutenant, we were almost immediately despatched to the north-west part of Ireland. The march extended to about 130 miles, and was accomplished in six days. The country through which we passed had more the appearance of a deserted than of a populous land; and had not the road been good, our expedition would have proved sufficiently irksome.

On the 1st of March, 1806, we left Dublin, the immediate environs of which are pretty good, but, after a few miles were passed, we began to remark a most sensible alteration. The contrast I before alluded to was here again perceptible, although in a different way, for the rich soil and picturesque scenery were in anything but harmony with the mud-cabins, which appeared to be the prevailing form of Irish habitations. The people all looked sullen and dejected; and the cows and sheep were the only living creatures which bore any semblance of English good feeding.

In the course of the day we reached the small town of Killcock, where we were received into houses destitute both of tables and chairs! and from hence, proceeding onwards, and finding little difference in the features of the landscape, we arrived in the evening at Kinnegad, County Westmeath, where the accommodations turned out to be something better. Here and there on the road we perceived sundry dilapidated cottages, whose dreary appearance bore ample testimony to the wild and ruinous scenes of the Irish rebellion.

On the 5th day, having continued our march over a desolate-looking moorland country, we arrived at Athlone, County Galway, which is said to be one of the largest towns in Ireland, although containing only about six hundred houses. The barracks, constructed for the use of artillery and infantry, were the best-looking buildings in the town, and here I met, for the first time since leaving Dublin, with a military force. We were invited to join the mess of the English officers, but for which act of courtesy, on their parts, our fare would have been indifferent. As it was, however, we did exceedingly well, especially with respect to wines, which they had procured of first-rate quality.

The following day, we resumed our dismal journey, and the country, instead of improving, appeared to grow worse and worse. We now rarely encountered even a solitary mud-hut, and the whole scene presented little else than a collection of huge blocks of stone, covered with moss. The inscription over the door of a public-house which we made a brief halt at struck me as being of a very singular character, namely, "Dry Lodgings!" leaving the traveller to suppose that such a luxury as preservation from humidity was scarcely to be calculated upon in an Irish inn.

At Ballinamore we stopped for the night; but really the houses of refreshment wore such a dilapidated appearance that it seemed quite hazardous to venture within side them; nor would anything have induced me to do so but the dreary alternative of bivouacking under a very threatening sky,

Indeed it is scarcely possible to describe the marks of poverty and utter destitution visible every mile we travelled in this island, which is evidently destined by nature for a much better fate. As we marched by, the wretched natives sauntered to the doors of their still more wretched huts, and gazed stupidly at the passing cavalcade. Miserable-looking horses, or rather asses, were here and there to be seen, with rude panniers thrown across them, filled with turf, &c. and tied together by ropes of straw.

At length, after a very fatiguing journey, we arrived at Dunamore, the place of our destination, which, from various accounts, as well as from its sounding name, I had been led to imagine was a place of some note. As it turned out, however, my expectations were completely baffled, since the town comprised only about some twenty or thirty brick houses, and a corresponding number of mud cottages. The church and church-steeple were quite covered with ivy.

Our arrival occasioned the assemblage of a whole host of ragged natives, who gazed on us with a-feeling apparently half friendly and half hostile. Our barracks had been formerly a gentleman's country house, and proved tolerably comfortable; the furniture was, however, of a true Irish character. A multitude of crows, which had established their quarters in the surrounding trees, disturbed by the bustle of our approach, became as noisy as possible—I suppose, in the spirit of sympathy.

Thus terminated our progress from Portsmouth to Dunamore, which had occupied the term of two months; and so little cause had I for satisfaction, either in the country through which I bad passed or the town wherein I was now stationed, that I conceived it absolutely impossible I could hold it out above a week! Little, however, are we aware of our own power of endurance.

The climate of this part of "green Erin" is mild, but damp; and seldom is a day to be met with which presents a cloudless sky. The landholders, and other opulent persons, seem by common consent to have abandoned this unfortunate island; and either Dublin, or the overgrown English capital, receives both them and the money which they extort from the hapless tenantry.

An Irish hut, though a good deal talked about, is perhaps not very clearly conceived, even by an Englishman. Its dimensions are usually from six to eight feet in height, and about twelve in circumference: it is thatched with straw, above which is generally laid a coat of turf. The light is admitted through a rode aperture, stopped up in bad weather; in one corner of the interior is a straw bed for the Christian part of the family: in another, a similar receptacle for a large sow and her little offspring; to these inmates are often added a goat, an ass, or some other quadruped; and the remainder of the hut is occupied by a broken table, a three-legged stool, and a spinning-wheel. Around the turf-fire are gathered the owner of the mansion, his wife and children—the happy pair deeply engaged in imbibing the fumes of the fragrant weed. The hole appropriated to exit and entrance is constructed so low, that the visitor must crouch almost double in order to gain admittance.

In this same melancholy town of Dunamore, there sure two churches—a Protestant and a Catholic one,—but neither of them has a peal of bells. The very graves in the churchyards partake of the rude character of the people—consisting merely of heaps of unhewn stones. If anybody of particular note is to be consigned to earth, an immense block of stone is raised over his remains; but as to inscriptions, nothing of the kind appears.

It is the custom, both in this country and in England, for the residents of a place to pay the first visit to a stranger. It was, therefore, with high gratification that I received the cards of the minister, and of a military officer who had just returned from the Continent and had a seat in the neighbourhood. The intercourse which sprang herefrom was, indeed, under my forlorn circumstances, agreeable in the extreme.

Whitsuntide, which in Germany I had been accustomed to observe with reverence and self-denial, was celebrated here with feelings the very reverse; and that, although Ireland is a Catholic country. On Whit Monday, a fair was held in the town for the sale of yarn, and on the following day succeeded a cattle-show, of a very indifferent character as to the exhibition of four-footed animals, and a very peculiar one as regarded their biped proprietors. The latter, indeed, however their bargaining might terminate, seemed resolved to grow merry; and proceeding from one step to another, became at length unable to move at all-dropping down very affectionately by the side of their beloved whisky-casks.

On others, it is true, this potent beverage took a different effect, rendering them noisy and quarrelsome; and hence it became necessary for the military power to be called in, to prevent bloodshed. This circumstance gave me opportunity to observe another peculiarity of the Irish character. When the ringleaders of the disturbance had been secured and were led before the magistrate, they fell on their knees and implored "mercy" in the most abject terms:—a mode of conduct never pursued in England, where an offender often braves the gallows itself with imperturbable fortitude.

About ten miles from Dunamore lies the more considerable town of Tuam. Hither business occasionally led me, and in its vicinity I saw, for the first time in this part of the country, a plough used. Its construction, however, was so clumsy, particularly as it was without wheels, that two horses, assisted by all the power of three men, were barely sufficient to drag it along. Towards the end of August the harvest commenced; but for carrying on this important agricultural labour no other implement was employed than a small sickle. The bundles of corn, when reaped, were borne home on the backs of the labourers, and afterwards threshed, with huge bludgeons, on a large stone.

By the end of September, the dense masses of cloud, and the increasing cold, contributed to render our quarters more cheerless than ever; and I was accordingly much pleased at the communication of orders to join the greater body of our regiment at Ballinrobe, about twenty miles off, from which place I took occasion to visit Castlebar, where the French general Humbert had, some years previously, made his unsuccessful descent.

On the 9th of November, intelligence reached us, in this obscure nook, of the fatal termination of the battle of Jena, whereby all hopes seemed to be destroyed, for the present, of revisiting our native country. The proverb says, that "misfortunes seldom come singly;" and the truth of it was in this instance illustrated, for a succession of storms and deluging rains set in, which latter, eventually, not only soaked through the roof of our barracks but actually sapped their foundations, rendering the lodgement unsafe as well as incommodious. Our people, unused to this kind of weather, soon drooped under its pestiferous effects; and dysentery (to which one of my brother-officers fell a victim) attacked the regiment to a very alarming extent. It will readily be imagined that these circumstances did not tend to enliven our local ennui.

After having witnessed an election for two members of parliament at Ballinrobe, which gave rise to infinite confusion and innumerable broken heads, I was instigated to visit the famous subterranean lakes situated about eight or nine miles from that town. We descended some twenty-five feet below the surface of the earth, and, on inspection, found these streams, which are said to empty themselves into the Atlantic Ocean, from twelve to eighteen feet in breadth. Their course is serpentine, but owing to the small portion of light which we could command it was difficult to trace them far.

In the month of February, 1807, I received an invitation to visit a gentleman's country-house in the neighbourhood: and here, although there was abundance of solid comforts, amounting to absolute profusion, the negligent habits of the country retained their influence, and were conspicuous in the dilapidated appearance of the mansion—the bed and window curtains of the sleeping-rooms being, although rich in material, dirty and ragged.

It is impossible not to be struck with the evidences of hardihood displayed by the Irish peasantry. Nothing is commoner than to find them travelling almost an incredible distance in one day unsupported by anything but a roasted potato or two and an occasional drink from a spring. In winter the children run about, with infinite glee, barefooted, upon the ice and snow.

At length, in the beginning of June, it was intimated that we should forthwith quit Ireland, although the point of our destination remained concealed. We suspected, however, that it was Sweden, in which country a corps of. English troops (together with a division of our legion) was stationed. On the 10th of June we actually did leave this desolate Ballinrobe, (apparently to the great regret of the inhabitants,) and taking the same direction by which we had travelled to it, found ourselves once more on the road to Dublin.

Chapter 9

Peace of Tilsit

On the evening of the 18th of June, 1807, I sailed, in company with the last division of my regiment, from the Irish capital. The beautiful harbour was thronged with boats and the shore with spectators; and the shouts of the people responded to the lively notes of our music. A passage of thirty-six hours (wind and weather being favourable) wafted us back to the bustling, opulent port of Liverpool, where we awaited further orders, for the arrival whereof we felt extremely anxious.

The division to which I was attached received directions to pursue its march by way of Warrington, Bolton, and Rochdale; and, subsequently, through a most bewitching country, to Halifax, in Yorkshire: hill and dale combined, in this fruitful district to invest the scenery with never-ceasing variety, and meadows of the most luxuriant herbage enclosed cattle which looked the very pictures of health and frolicsome enjoyment. Large manufactories every now and then displayed themselves, and reminded the traveller of the industry and wealth which rendered the region flourishing in artificial as well as natural advantages.

But, strangely enough, all this was contrasted with a clumsy boorish look, and roughness of apparel, on the part of the people, rarely to be met with in other English provinces—a remark, by the by, which obtrudes itself pretty generally whilst one is traversing a manufacturing region; and from which the deduction arises that, to the mass of the community, agriculture is a more productive employment than artisanship.

From Halifax, we proceeded to the important city of Leeds, which is of immense size, and contains a great number of manufactories. Thence our course led us to York, the capital of the province. This is a large and populous city, but the streets are inconveniently narrow, and many of the houses and public buildings wear a very antiquated appearance.

The cathedral, or minster, is by far the most interesting object here, ranking next to St. Paul's in magnitude. The interior of this edifice is exceedingly venerable and majestic, and encloses many fine monuments. The exterior, is elaborately adorned with sculptures, on which, however, the hand of Time has wrought its customary dilapidation. The sultriness and exceeding drought which we had hitherto experienced during our march from Liverpool made us fancy ourselves quite in another climate, when we recollected the constant dampness and frequent rains of Ireland.

On the 30th of June, we quitted York, after two days' halt, in the direction of Pocklington, from whence we marched to Beverley, and remained there until the 26th of July. The cause assigned for this protracted sojourn was, that we might await the conclusion of the truce of Tilsit, which, as is well known, terminated in a peace between Napoleon and Alexander, whereupon the British government proceeded to fit out their contemplated expedition, the precise object of which was, however, still involved in obscurity.

During the early part of our stay in this neighbourhood, we underwent considerable apprehension, owing to the anticipated pacific measures of Russia, that our services would be altogether unnecessary,—more especially, as it was obvious that Sweden (to which our eyes had been directed) would offer no longer a theatre for our exertions.

It was, therefore, with no small surprise that we received, on the 26th of July, orders for embarking the next day at Hull; intelligence which, however agreeable it might be to some, was to many of us, who had little encouragement, under the present aspect of things, to return to the Continent, rather irksome than otherwise;—more particularly as we found ourselves here in capital quarters, and in the daily receipt of pleasant convivial invitations. By the commander-in-chief of the district, especially, we were treated with uncommon hospitality. This veteran soldier had served in Germany during the famous seven years' war, and was additionally endeared to us by still retaining some smattering of the German tongue. On our departure, his concern really amounted almost to the paternal.

Chapter 10

Surrender of the Danish Fleet

On the 28th of July, 1807, we embarked at Hull; the preparations for which event seemed to imply the probability of a long voyage. On the 30th of the same month, thirty-six transport-ships left the harbour, containing our regiment amongst others; and having been joined by our convoy, (consisting of the *Defence*, 74 guns, and a man of war which had been captured from the French,) and subsequently by another squadron of transports under similar protection, we made sail for the Baltic on the morning of the 1st of August. By the 8th of that month we beheld the island of Anhalt on our right, and to the left the Swedish coast.

On the evening of this day the weather, which had hitherto been favourable, became rough; and towards night the heavens were disturbed by one of the most tremendous storms it has ever been my lot to witness. Hail, wind, lightning, and thunder, combined to lash the furies of the deep into horrible commotion. In the western sky the light of departing day still lingered, whilst the eastern horizon was shrouded in black masses. The quickly repeated flashes disclosed, to our no small astonishment, a very considerable addition to our fleet, and occasionally Helsingborg and the castle of Helsingoer half presented themselves by the same fearful illumination.

The increasing breeze howled and screeched amongst our rigging; the waves beat over the decks; and amidst this tremendous uproar our commodore greeted, with a discharge of cannon, an admiral's flag-ship, which, it appeared, had just arrived in the roads and speedily returned his salute.

Under these circumstances did we enter the roads of Helsingoer. The signal was given for anchoring; in the same moment the wind shifted and the gate blew stronger than ever, and it was fully midnight before the cessation of the storm enabled our vessel to cast anchor and the sailors to recreate themselves after their exertions with a supply of liquid very different from that wherewith during the last few hours their bodies had been drenched.

The morning which succeeded this tempestuous night (Sunday, August 9th) was clear and calm. I went upon deck, and was quite surprised at the beautiful sight which met my eyes. About 400 English ships of war and transport vessels had gradually collected together, and Helsingoer and Helsingborg lay completely in view.

I soon after accompanied our captain to the former place, which, in its general aspect and style of buildings, bears some resemblance to the English towns; but one misses greatly the commodious pavements of the latter, as well as the prevailing air of comfort and opulence. We dined at an English merchant's, where a large company was assembled, but no member of it could solve the mystery of our appearance here, although upon this circumstance the discourse almost wholly turned.

In the evening we returned on board, and the object of our expedition now began to develop itself. Orders arrived prohibiting any further intercourse with the shore; and next day our vessel took a station more removed from Helsingoer castle.

On the 13th instant, all the boats belonging to the transport-ships were examined and directed to be kept in readiness at a minute's notice. A supply of two days' provisions was likewise cooked and distributed amongst the troops; all which circumstances combined to forebode immediate landing. A report now spread that the purpose of the English government was to possess itself forcibly of Zealand and the Danish fleet, as a negotiation which had been carried on with the view of acquiring these peaceably had failed; in the apprehension of which failure, the squadron of Sir Richard Keates had, for some previous time, been so stationed as to prevent the possibility of any assistance being despatched from Holstein.

The entire British land force accumulated for this enterprise amounted to about 15,000 men, and the combined effect of their several military bands, sounding upon the water, was at once agreeable and imposing. They played for an hour or two every evening; the signal for ceasing being given from the admiral's flag-ship and repeated by every other vessel. After dusk, the fleet assumed a very picturesque appearance, not much dissimilar from that of an illuminated town; each vessel displaying a lantern and various other lights.

Although extremely near both the Danish and Swedish coasts, yet as all communication was interdicted, we felt no small privation from the want of fresh provisions, and more especially of water, our supply of which necessary article was, owing to the heat of the weather, particularly bad. Our vessel lay accidentally close alongside the admiral's ship, the *Prince of Wales,* a three-decker, of 130 guns:—hence, I had an opportunity of observing that the commands issued on board a man-of-war are attended to with far greater precision than on board any other vessel.

On the 15th of August, orders were issued for weighing anchor, and towards the afternoon of that day we were in full sail for the capital of Denmark —the towers of which rose upon our view within an hour. Sailing by the small island of Huen, we anchored in the vicinity of Hellerup, where we remained stationary for three days, during which interval every preparation was made for landing.

The 18th of August, 1807, was the eventful day whereon the greater part of our armament was disembarked; the light infantry and part of the cavalry taking the lead. The position of the British fleet was about two gunshots from an island just opposite the height of the village of Hellerup, (upon which stood numerous large country-houses) and about ten miles from Copenhagen itself. Day was just beginning to break when I was called upon deck to witness this striking scene; Much noise and confusion prevailed around, proceeding from the numberless boats which were gradually filling with soldiers, but still keeping close to the transport-ships until the whole were ready.

To cover the landing, two gun-boats were sent in very close to shore, and upon a given signal several hundred boats pushed off from the respective transport-ships and made with all rapidity for land: In each boat were from twenty to thirty soldiers, &c.; they were severally towed by still smaller craft wherein sat the officers. Within the next hour I could already perceive, marching up the shore, a whole line of infantry; and to our utter astonishment, no opposition whatever was offered by the Danes, although with the help of telescopes we could discern in the distance bodies of their cavalry. By ten o'clock, a. m. ten thousand men had effected a landing, and formed themselves upon the height of Hellerup. In the afternoon, 100 hussars, with their horses, together with the horses of the light-artillery and of the staff-officers, were disembarked.

The pacific-minded Danish Monarch and his high-spirited son, the crown prince (now king), had retired by the Belt, with their court, from the scene of action, although undergoing thereby some risk of capture. Two princesses had however remained behind, in the capital, but were promptly accommodated with English passports to enable them to join their friends.

Next morning, by break of dawn, the army marched, in three columns, direct to Copenhagen, throwing back all the Danish outposts. The enemy's gun-boats did, it is true, meanwhile appear, and fired upon the left wing of the advancing forces, but were soon driven back into the harbour by the English brigs and bomb-ships. On the following day, when they again ventured out, they were fired on by our troops from the shore, who likewise overthrew a division of Danish forces which had attempted to occupy the high road, driving them back into the city. The result of this affair was the capture of one of the suburbs.

At the landing-place near Charlottenlund, a strong party of seamen was engaged in hauling ashore sundry battering engines, to be used in the siege, whilst Copenhagen was beleaguered on all sides; Major-General Von Peymann having the chief command of its garrison.

On the 24th, when the Danish troops at length seemed disposed to show themselves in good earnest, the assailants nevertheless succeeded in obtaining possession of the suburbs on the northern shore, upon which occasion Sir Arthur Wellesley, with his division, particularly distinguished themselves. The Danes had endeavoured to fire these suburbs, in which design they were only partially successful, and in truth little would have been gained by them had they been more so, since the English immediately changed their line of attack.

I rode on the 26th to Yägersburg, about ten miles from the metropolis. My route lay through the royal gardens at Friederichsburg, where the infantry and cavalry of our legion were in cantonments. The horses were fastened to the trees, and the men had erected straw huts. The battalion to which I belonged, however, was quartered in barracks at Yägersburg. I was billeted in the house of an old lady who had not joined in the flight of her neighbours. The poor creature was full of terror, and informed me that at the time of our landing, and upon the advance of the Scottish infantry, all the other inhabitants had either deserted the place or had concealed themselves and locked their doors. These latter precautions, however, were quite unavailing—the houses being opened by force.

Meanwhile preparations for the siege of Copenhagen were in active progress: when, on the 26th, it was announced that the Danish General Kastenskiold, supported by General Oxholm, with a body composed partly of regular troops and partly of militia hastily assembled, was marching to relieve the capital. Hence it became necessary to detach an English corps, in order to frustrate this movement; for which purpose one division was selected, under General Von Linsingen, comprising three light dragoon regiments, a battery of mounted artillery, the 95th English regiment of light infantry, &c. and another, consisting of the reserve of the army, (which advanced from the coast,) under Sir

Arthur Wellesley.

We marched during extremely hot weather and oppressed by many privations, until very late in the night, and then usually encamped before villages, where (according to circumstances) we either constructed rude huts with whatever materials were to be gathered in the surrounding fields, or took possession of the nearest houses and sheds. Provisions, indeed, we compelled the inhabitants to find us, but had frequently to fetch them ourselves, whence arose numerous disorders incidental to a state of warfare, notwithstanding strict discipline was enjoined. We had no means of transporting supplies from one place to another.

After passing three days on this disagreeable march, we reached Roeskilde, or Roskilkroe, the place of interment for the Danish princes. This town is one of the oldest in the kingdom, and is romantically situated, although in itself it contains nothing either of beauty or interest. I here received a voluntary offer of quarters from a lady who had been formerly attached to the Danish court, as she expressed the most groundless terrors at the English who accompanied us, and hoped to receive through me, a German, some little indulgences.

We had expected to have come up with the Danish militia at this place, but now learned that they had taken a position at Kiöge, and intended there to await their enemy. Sir Arthur Wellesley, upon receiving this intelligence, decided on proceeding to attack them, and concerted measures with General Von Linsingen for the latter to cross the intervening stream and thus get into the enemy's flank, whilst he (Sir Arthur) attacked them in front.

On the 29th of August both divisions put themselves in motion in order to effect a junction at the point agreed upon. Towards noon our corps arrived at the stream in question, which was at no great distance from Kiöge, and found the bridge, as might have been anticipated, broken up. Although the river turned out to be fordable, yet some delay occurred in consequence of tins, whereby Sir Arthur was led to apprehend that our general had failed in his part of the enterprise. Nevertheless he did not hesitate in assailing the enemy, who received him with a cannonade; and no sooner had our division crossed the river than the infantry at once found themselves in the thickest of the action.

The Danes ultimately retreated behind their trenches on the north side of the town, still endeavouring, however, to keep up the contest with their cavalry, and striving to turn the flank of the 92nd Regiment, which had pursued them; but Sir Arthur outmanoeuvred them in this point, and they were eventually driven out of their trenches and fled in disorder into the streets of the town. The two English divisions now made their junction, and unitedly pursued the enemy, who sought to rally in the churchyard of Kiöge, from whence, however, our artillery soon dislodged them.

The fugitives having been followed up about five or six miles, we encountered, in and near the village of Herfolgen, another Danish force, headed by General Oxholm, second-in-command of the hostile army. This was also posted chiefly in the churchyard of the place; and the English cannonade being directed against the church steeple, apprehension of its fall quickly induced the enemy to surrender. Here and there a small party, or a single soldier, still continued a running fire, when a truce was concluded; and on the arrival of Sir Arthur Wellesley, the swords of the capitulating officers were given up to him.

In this village, which apprehension at our approach had caused to be well nigh deserted, we halted—the few people who remained (consisting chiefly of women and children) having crept into various hiding-corners, expecting nothing less than death in case of discovery by our troops, although no kind of harm was projected towards their persons.

Whatever could be found in the way of provisions was undoubtedly appropriated; nor will it appear matter of surprise that, in the ranks of an invading army, individuals should be included capable of committing still further spoliation. By degrees the terror of these poor people subsided; and, on the second day of our encampment, their women came confidently about us soliciting bread.

On the third day we quitted this forlorn hamlet, which a week before had been wrapt in profound tranquillity. After marching two miles, we arrived at the small town of Ringstedt, which place had been burnt down the previous year, but had been, for the greater part, subsequently rebuilt. Here also the inhabitants displayed considerable alarm, particularly as a corps of militia had been organised here, on which account they conceived it likely that we might visit them with additional severity.

I was quartered with the family of a medical gentleman who had joined this militia; and, as he had been taken prisoner, the aversion of his wife to receive any of us was extreme, notwithstanding our repeated assurances that there was nothing to dread. Her vociferous grief was indeed of such a nature as to remain indelibly impressed on my memory; and yet, next morning, no sooner had the band of our regiment begun to play than the cheerful sound appeared to create in her a wondrous revulsion of feeling, and warfare, husband and all were forgotten in admiration of a few wind instruments! A few days after, the man returned to her longing arms safe and sound.

After a lapse of three days, a part of our corps resumed its pursuit of the Danes, and with the intent of seizing whatever arms they might find. As the infantry was transported upon wagons, the ground was got over quickly, and we shortly reached the little town of Nestved, in the meadows surrounding which we bivouacked. The whole of our detachment consisted of two thousand men, for whom the inhabitants were obliged to provide provisions. Walking through the streets of this place, I inquired for a public-house, upon which a tradesman's shop was pointed out to me.

I entered doubtingly; but the housekeeper confirmed the report, and regaled me plentifully, appearing very anxious to learn whether any sacking of the town was likely to ensue. I replied, by assuring him that the question even was offensive to the character of English troops—and, as I found myself very comfortable, strengthened their confidence by proposing to remain their guest until the departure of our division—whereupon they immediately expressed themselves at ease.

Pursuing our route five Danish miles further, we arrived at the coasting town of Wordingborg, where our infantry took up their quarters in the abandoned dwelling-houses, whilst a body of militia which had been stationed in the place took to their vessels a couple of hours previous to our arrival.

The enemy appearing now to be completely dislodged, we returned to Nestved, and from thence, after an interval of two days, proceeded to Corsoer, a very pretty town situated on the borders of the Great Belt. Stopping here likewise two days, for the purpose of seeking and appropriating all the arms we could get at, we next went, on the 8th of September, to Slagelse. The weather had now become very sharp; a circumstance which it is fortunate had not happened sooner—as our people would have suffered greatly bivouacking under the canopy of Heaven.

Whilst we were thus engaged in marching from place to place, driving the Danish military before us, and disarming the natives, the British force lying before Copenhagen was not less active. By the end of August, they had so far completed their preparations for the siege as to be warranted in summoning the capital to surrender, which step was taken on the 1st of September by the respective commanders of the land and sea forces—Admiral Gambier and General Cathcart. As the answer to this summons was unsatisfactory, purporting the determination of the besieged to await the decision of their king, the bombardment of the city by the united services commenced on the 2nd instant, and was answered, though faintly, by the garrison.

The fire soon spread rapidly amongst the buildings of the ill-fated metropolis; and in the hope that this specimen of the horrors of war would produce the desired effect, our commanders suspended the bombardment on the night of the 4th instant. This circumstance, however, occasioned the besieged to fall into a fatal error, by imagining the slackened fire of the assailants to result from want of ammunition—and, accordingly, they redoubled their resistance. Hence, the bombardment was renewed without loss of time, and that with so much vigour as to bring down the steeple of the principal church! Horror and devastation now spread widely around. Bombs, Congreve-rockets, and cannon-balls were poured unintermittingly into the devoted city—and nowhere could the affrighted citizens ensure their safety. Many of them strove to escape to Amack.

On the 5th of September, the Danish commandant demanded a truce for twenty-four hours, in order to make propositions: but this was peremptorily refused, and the unconditional surrender of the Danish fleet required as a preliminary to any negotiation. However, the firing was discontinued meanwhile, and on the 6th the enemy held a council of war, the majority of voices whereat decided not to subject the capital to further demolition, but close with the terms of the invaders.

Lord Cathcart having summoned Sir Arthur Wellesley, (who had throughout greatly distinguished himself,) they concluded, in conjunction with Sir Home Popham and Lieutenant-Colonel Murray, on the night between the 6th and 7th of September, the well-known capitulation, by virtue of which the Danish fleet and naval stores were given into the hands of England. It was also settled that the British forces should at the latest within six weeks withdraw.

It had been at one time projected by the enemy to burn their ships—an idea, however, which was quickly abandoned, as it seemed only calculated to increase their sufferings and peril; and thus this immense booty, consisting of upwards of sixty ships of war, of various sizes, (and in value exceeding 4,000,000 dollars,) with a prodigious quantity of naval stores, fell into the power of the British Government. The loss on the part of the Danes was reported to be from 1800 to 2000 men: on our side it was by no means so considerable.

The principal object was hereby attained of this expedition, which had made so much noise, and had given rise to so many speculations as to the views of Napoleon with respect to drawing Denmark into the war end increasing its naval advantages by means of her fleet. Upon this question I shall not presume to speak confidently; but it should be recollected that the policy of that extraordinary individual led him to make tools of every state over which his influence extended; under winch view of the case, England may be held excused for preventing in this instance so considerable an accession to her enemy's power.

I was now quartered in the village of Beingstrup, in the house of the clergyman, which being capacious, was burdened with eight officers and thirty privates. The necessary provision for this large party engrossed, as may be supposed, the labour and attention of the household: and scarcely had their assiduities commenced, before intelligence arrived to the wife of the minister that her brother had perished during the hostilities at Copenhagen—that her father's house in that city had been burnt down—and her brother-in-law killed in the skirmish near Kiöge! This distressing combination of misfortunes was well calculated to overwhelm the poor woman's heart and overflow her eyes: but the perpetual noise and rude confusion incidental to the nature of her guests, prevented the fall indulgence even of the latter mournful relief.

At the termination of six days I proceeded to Ringstedt, and two days after once mere entered Nestved, where our stay extended to sixteen days, during which time we lived on the best terms with the people of the town. But at length the ennui of our situation became almost insupportable, and one day whilst striving to dissipate it by turning over the leaves of La Fontaine's *Sonderling*, I was roused most agreeably by the roll of the ordnance through the street, and the trumpet-signal for mustering—and in a few hours bad already exchanged my snug quarters for others of a rougher description in a country hamlet This hasty breaking-up, as I subsequently understood, was in consequence of the reported landing on some parts of the island of Zealand of hostile forces—the Danish king not having hitherto ratified the capitulation.

Our next halt for any time was at the village of Utby; and whilst stopping here, I took occasion to visit Kallehaven, whereat there was a communication with the island of Moen, on which account it was strongly occupied by our troops. From an adjoining height, a very beautiful prospect is commanded;—the eye of the traveller wandering over the large island of Falster, which, together with a number of lesser ones thickly strewn with country houses and gardens, uplifts itself beneath from the bosom of ocean.

I had, in fact, an opportunity of thoroughly traversing the island of Zealand, which extends in length about seventy miles, and in breadth about forty-five. It is well cultivated, and requites the husbandman's care by returning him a plentiful harvest. At the season of my sojourn there, the face of nature wore a most delightful aspect. The manner of living practised by the inhabitants was liberal, and resembled the English rather than the German style, although the language of the latter country generally prevails.

On the 12th of October, instructions arrived to hold ourselves in readiness for embarkation, and the following day we departed from Utby. There was nothing very pleasant in the notion of this movement: inasmuch as exchanging the fine *terra firma,* whereon we had been stationed, for the dangerous passage of the Categat, at this advanced season of the year, was calculated rather to depress than to elevate the spirits; more especially in my instance, as I had contrived to form several agreeable acquaintanceships.

We found ourselves, on the 16th of October, within a very few miles of Copenhagen; and next morning, advanced (through one of the *faubourgs*, which had suffered great dilapidations from the hands of the Danes themselves) to the entrance of the capital. Here, however, our progress was impeded by a body of Danish cavalry, by which we were conducted, not through the metropolis, but round it, to the Holm; it having been stipulated that no English armed force should enter Copenhagen.

The harbour and the roads at Holm were praised by the English seamen, as amongst the most commodious in Europe. The place itself, at the same time, presented a desolate and ruinous appearance; many of the warehouses and wharfs being quite empty.

I had scarcely sufficient time to make a little excursion to Copenhagen, in order to provide myself with necessaries for the voyage before us. This, indeed, I found not very easy to accomplish, partly from a real scarcity of the articles I sought, and partly from the evident disinclination of the inhabitants to accommodate us. To speak truth, I had no desire to prolong my visit; for the objects around me, more especially the ruins of St. Mary's church, were sufficiently mournful, both to the eye and heart.

The stated period of the capitulation extended not beyond the morning of the 18th. The embarkation was accordingly expedited, as much as possible, and the confusion necessarily resulting is scarcely to be described.

Chapter 11

The "Tables Turned"

The 21st of October, 1807, was the memorable day whereon the fleet assembled in the roads before Copenhagen, exceeding, perhaps, in magnitude, any that had ever been previously collected together, got under weigh, and in the course of an hour was in full sail. It consisted of eighty English and Danish ships of war, of various sizes, with about 700 transport vessels.

Two hours subsequently, we entered the Strait between Helsingoer and Helsingborg, which places we greeted with a salute in passing, by way of respect to the King of Sweden, who was reported to be a visitor at his fortress, of, Helsingoer, for the, purpose of witnessing this splendid spectacle. It was a fine autumnal morning, and the whole scene was calculated to make an indelible, impression upon the minds more particularly of such as were unaccustomed to similar objects.

Having emerged from the Strait, orders were received by our captain to make all sail for Yarmouth; whereat some surprise was expressed, as we had speculated on harbouring in a Swedish port. The weather now grew unfavourable and boisterous; and it was not long before the unpleasant discovery was made that our vessel had sprung a leak. Hence it became necessary to set the pumps in motion at intervals of six hours, whereas, under ordinary circumstances, they are only worked every three days.

Before we had got out of the Categat, it blew a gale from the N.W.; but, as we were sailing between the Swedish and Danish coasts, we did not suffer much. On the afternoon of the 23rd, however, owing to our more exposed situation, the ill effects of the storm began to be demonstrated; and towards evening, manifested themselves completely by confusion of the most appalling and, at the same time, ludicrous kind.

The various articles in the cabins were hurled from one spot to another; doors torn from their hinges—tables and chairs reeling about as if disposed to strike up a dance; and, in the midst of this hubbub, I, whilst endeavouring to secure the door of our cabin, was fairly thrown at full length upon the planks forming part of that frail medium which intervened between us and destruction.

The calm which succeeded this gale continued upwards of three days, and was taken advantage of by the ship's carpenter to repair the leak. On the 26th of October, to our great satisfaction, the wind freshened from the north-east, and, going at the rate of from eight to ten knots, we quickly lost sight of the rest of the fleet, of which we saw nothing more during the remainder of the passage to Yarmouth, in the roads whereof we arrived on the night of the 28th. These roads are among the very worst in England, being exposed on all sides, and affording but a bad entrance to the harbour. In consequence of these disadvantages, vessels, excepting in case of necessity, seldom put in here.

The wind remaining against us, we lay at anchor for the space of eight days, on the second of which I went ashore, to relieve the tedium of confinement on board, and to procure fresh provisions, which were growing scanty.

As soon as circumstances permitted, we resumed our voyage, but were again unfortunate enough to encounter rough weather, during which one of the transports in our company was stranded on the rocky coast of Kent, and sank with her whole company, including from three hundred to four hundred men (infantry belonging to the German Legion). An empty bark, which had appertained to this vessel, was seen by us next morning riding about, in forlorn plight, upon the waves.

The wind still continuing contrary, and none of our convoy being in sight; we had some apprehensions of being driven too near the French coast, and falling into the hands of the enemy. Hence, our course was reversed; and in order to avoid this danger we steered back again to Yarmouth. Here our situation, although mended in one respect, was still perilous, in consequence of the continuance of the bad weather, whereby one of the Danish line-of-battle ships was dismasted, thrown upon a sandbank, and compelled to cast her cannons overboard. This vessel, which had on board a great number of soldiers, besides her own crew, presented, under these circumstances, a spectacle of the most melancholy description.

By the time we were at anchor in the Downs, the immense fleet which, on leaving Copenhagen, had almost literally covered the sea, was reduced to about fifty sail, the remainder having been separated in stress of weather or directed to different ports. On the 15th of November, we made for Ramsgate; and in due time found ourselves snugly quartered in the barracks at Deal, where we had the satisfaction to learn that our legion had sustained no other loss than that of the transport already mentioned, and where, amidst the comforts of *terra firma* security and good fare, we soon forgot the various dangers add privations of our tiresome voyage. At the end of the month orders were received, in pursuance whereof we repaired to the barracks at Weymouth.

Chapter 12

Military Precaution

We entered on our march of two hundred miles on the 30th of November, in cold and, rainy weather; and arrived on the same day at Canterbury, where I visited some old friends. From hence we proceeded, by Faversham, to Chatham, at which place I went to inspect the dock-yard; but, although dressed in uniform, I found it necessary, in the first place, to provide myself with a card of admission. Nelson's flag-ship (the *Victory*) lay here on the stocks undergoing repair; and I remarked with some curiosity the brass plate which had been let in to mark the spot whereon the hero stood at the moment of receiving the fatal ball.

At one of the inns of Basingstoke, we met with a true specimen of John Bull in the person of a violent declaimer against the "heavy taxes" under which Great Britain was labouring; and, benevolently desirous of alleviating his concern, we took an opportunity of explaining the extent and manner in which our native country was laid under contribution by the French: whereupon our malcontent brightened up amazingly, and left the room deeply impressed with a sense of the preference due to a system of taxation imposed by those who have a common interest in the country.

On our arrival at Weymouth, we were received by the good citizens, as well as by the people of the surrounding neighbourhood, with great kindness and cordiality; the more especially as it is well known that, after active service, much is always requisite towards putting in good order the accoutrements and appointments of a body of military, and consequently employment given to a number of hands. The barracks had, during our absence, been enlarged.

The 18th of January, 1808, (being the birthday of the Queen,) the Dragoon Regiments were drawn up on parade, previously to which, however, jackets trimmed with fur had been distributed, which gave our men the appearance of hussars. A gay uniform is, indeed, a great point with the English in their estimate of military men; and some of their cavalry-officers have so great a consciousness of the finery wherewith they are invested, as to occasion their spreading an umbrella while on horseback, in order to screen it from humidity![1]

Up to the middle of May, my regiment remained at Weymouth, and then repaired to Wareham, from which place we did not depart until the 9th of February in the following year, when we proceeded to Ipswich.

Although the good people of Wareham appeared to regret our leaving them, their regret was by no means strongly expressed: indeed, it is not etiquette in England to express any emotion powerfully; their feelings seem all to be kept in abeyance. A shake of the hand, accompanied by "I am glad to see you," or, "I am sorry to part from you," is the utmost one Englishman concedes to another.

About this period, the English government made strenuous efforts to repair the losses that had been sustained by their troops during the unfortunate Spanish campaign which terminated at Corunna; and with this view a bounty of thirty guineas was offered to any recruit. Contrary to expectation, the German Legion received orders early in April, 1860, to march to Portsmouth, and embark from that place for Portugal—an event the less anticipated by us, inasmuch as we had just arrived from the

1. Nothing is more common on the Continent, than to quiz our martial fellow-countrymen at masquerades, &c for this and other specimens of coxcombry. The writer of this note has frequently, at fancy balls, encountered whimsical mimicries of the English warlike *petit-maîtres.*

southern parts of England. The French forces, meanwhile, had taken possession of the greater part of Portugal; but as a fresh treaty had been Recently concluded between that country and Great Britain, which latter had likewise entered into an alliance with the Junta of Spain,—Sir Arthur Wellesley having possession of Lisbon and the right bank of the Tagus,—it appeared, all circumstances considered, that the Peninsula war would now be persevered in with more energy than ever.

On the 11th of April, accordingly, we quitted Ipswich, and in order to ensure despatch, and avoid burdening the public-houses on the line of march, were separated into several divisions, and took two different roads. So great, in fact, was the celerity of our movements, that we performed the whole distance by forced marches, and, on reaching Portsmouth, were conducted to the several transports without any halt whatever: indeed, had the wind served, I doubt not we should have weighed anchor without the least loss of time. As it was, however, we were detained in the harbour until next day, whereby I gained an opportunity of going ashore, and making sundry useful purchases.

Next day the whole squadron, destined for Portugal, stood out to sea, and lay-to in the roads off Spithead. This anchorage (between the Isle of Wight and. the mainland of Great Britain) is exceedingly commodious, extends several leagues both in length and breadth, and has two outlets to the ocean. Having awaited here, during fourteen days, the joining of other transports, also filled with soldiers, our armament was, at length, considered complete, and we immediately made further sail.

Chapter 13

Feast of the Ascension

Our voyage was not particularly rapid, and it was the 5th of May when we discerned the snow-covered points of certain high mountains, a sight from which our seamen inferred that we were between Oporto and Lisbon. In the course of the voyage, we had steered so close to the commodore's ship, as to enable his hailing us with his speaking-trumpet, and directing our master not to make directly for Lisbon, but to proceed to the mouth of the Mondego, and disembark the troops there,—our regiment being destined to act in conjunction with the English commander. Little as this intelligence removed the uncertainty which, necessarily hung over the affairs of the Peninsula, it gave to us token of speedy conflict; and our men proceeded, with infinite gusto, to sharpen their warlike instruments upon the grinding-stones of the ship. Wind and weather were favourable for landing, and the sails being furled, we speedily reached the coast.

On the evening of the 6th of May, we lay at anchor at the mouth of the Mondego, and, directly after, the masters of the different vessels having been ordered to attend the commodore for instructions, it turned out that our regiment was to land the following day. From the deck of our transport-ship, we could observe Buarcos, a small place, the houses whereof looked quite grey, and were built in the most irregular style. The surrounding country appeared both rocky and sandy, and was strewn, here and there, with pine-trees.

Not having heard, for the space of fourteen days, how matters stood, we could not avoid feeling particularly anxious; and our impatience rose to an extreme height, when it was found impracticable to disembark on the following day, as projected. The necessary preparations were, however, made, and the Portuguese boats soon came about us, laden with fine oranges, bread, and wine, for sale. The heavens had been clear during the last five days, and the weather warm, although every afternoon a stiff gale blew from land, which brought on fog, and rendered the atmosphere disagreeable.

Five of the transports (having on board a battalion of our regiment) had parted company, and probably, not observing the signals to the contrary, had proceeded to Lisbon.

At length, on the 8th of May, commenced our disembarkation, to effect which, the vessels were compelled to advance as nearly as possible to shore. I could not however manage to quit the ship before next morning, about eight o'clock, when I stepped for the first time upon Portuguese ground—not, by-the-by, without having experienced a thorough ducking, no boat being able to approach the landing-place sufficiently near to enable a man to spring upon dry land. But how sudden and how great was the effect produced upon my feelings by this introduction to a southern climate! In the temperature, the difference was most striking. About ten days before, only, we had left the English coast clad in the habiliments of winter, which we were here compelled at once to cast aside.

On board, sea and sky combined to produce a sharp air and thereby to lessen considerably the degree of the heat, but on land it was absolutely oppressive! Nevertheless, one breathes here more freely than in northern climates; and the plants which in the hothouses of colder lands are stunted and weakly, shoot up without care or sickliness even from a sandy soil.

The houses of the small town of Buarcos are constructed principally of rock-stone, and have few windows, in order that the glare of the sun may, as much as possible, be excluded. The natives of the place, whom curiosity had led to gape at our disembarkation, presented a singular contrast, particularly in point of costume, to the English. They seemed to be a slender race, with yellow complexions, and great indolence of manner. The poorer classes were uniformly barefooted, though, in spite of the intense, heat, they were covered with mantles!—and to motions slow and relaxed united a style of speaking at once ready and energetic. Altogether, the observation was forcibly impressed upon my mind that in a climate such as this the anxiety of man must be comparatively slight to provide efficient means of sustaining and even of indulging life.

No sooner were our horses saddled, than I rode off half a league to Figueiras to join that part of our regiment which had landed the preceding day and was already in quarters there. This town lies at the mouth of the Mondego, and in my progress thither, I found the sultriness excessive: the road was deeply covered with sand. Passing by the battery which commanded the entrance of the river, but was miserably constructed, we rode into the town, the streets whereof appeared to be in a most wretched plight, and were rendered additionally gloomy by the shadow cast from houses five or six stories high.

In the market lay many fellows who had gone thither for purposes of traffic, both to buy and sell, wrapt up in their dark-blue mantles, seemingly quite heedless of everything going on around them. The gentlemen of the town walked about in huge great coats, whilst the ladies sought refuge from the heat which their gallants apparently courted, by the use of immense parasols.

In discovering my quarters, I found my knowledge of French of considerable utility; and the master of the house received me kindly, taking care to provide everything that was comfortable. He lost no time in ordering for me a plentiful breakfast after the English fashion, though the dinner which followed was rather *à la Française,* namely, consisting of much soup, abundance of vegetables, and very little meat. The most costly part of the affair was the dessert, which consisted, amongst other things, of exquisite oranges such as are not to be met with in Germany or

England at any price. That evening the town was illuminated, in honour of our arrival; and everyone who had the means decorated the front of his house with a number of lamps;—nor was the compliment expressed by this the only agreeable thing to us, as we were consequently enabled with far more ease, to find our way about the narrow and ill-paved thoroughfares of this strange town.

The feast of the ascension was not celebrated at Figueiras with pomp equal to that which I have witnessed in other Catholic lands. Nevertheless, it attracted a good many country people, who chiefly rode into the town upon mules, &c. When they had arrived, however, they seemed in no hurry to go to church, only taking pious care to pop in at the critical moment of the priest raising the Host, and at other parts of the day stretching themselves listlessly upon the earth, and resembling in their want of shoes and general raggedness of garb the lower orders of Irish. The number of alms-begging fiddlers and cymbal-players was prodigious! but of monks, (considering the size of the place,) I saw but few.

The poorer classes live principally on loaves made from Indian or Turkish corn, which in Portugal is a good deal patronised. The bread made from this material has rather a sweetish taste and is not easy of digestion. The straw is appropriated as fodder for cattle, which purpose it answers extremely well, and is therefore in much esteem.

The mustering of our regiment occasioned a great deal of curiosity: the people admiring particularly our English horses, which contrasted very strikingly with the mules in constant use amongst the Portuguese. The vineyards hereabouts did not come up to my anticipations. The ground indeed, generally speaking, is negligently cultivated. Little attention is paid to cleanliness in Figueiras, and I may add throughout Portugal; in fact, every kind of unspeakable filth issues from the windows into the streets (to the manifest danger of the passer-by) where the horror is suffered to remain until cleared by swine and dogs, or washed away by the happy intermediation of a heavy shower.

I could not help being amused with the inordinate use of snuff amongst these people; and, as for their mode of dining, it was really quite startling to a stranger to observe the rapidity with which their food was swallowed after it had been mixed and mashed into a sort of solid soup. By a curious inversion of the common order of things, the better classes of Portuguese are far the most active.

They pass a good deal of time in promenading about, whilst the tradesman is much slower in his movements, and the mechanic scarcely moves at all!—so that, in proportion to the necessity of exertion, is apparently the want of it! In fact, the necessaries of the Portuguese labourer or peasant are not many; he cares not for shoes, and consequently there are but few who practise the gentle craft of St. Crispin; he is contented with mere rags as garments, (which he can hide, upon occasion, under his mantle,) and hence the number of knights of the yard and thimble is dolefully scanty.

Many citizens lounge through the whole day on seats before their doors, or lie stretched upon the ground, which latter employment is an exceedingly favourite one amongst the lowest classes, who hesitate not, in the most public spots, to commence a diligent search after the vermin by which their tawny carcases are invaded. To turn to the reverse of the medal;—these people are good-natured, and were, at the time of which I speak, particularly so towards us, hoping by our means to be delivered from the tyranny of the French.

Contrary to expectation, we remained at Figueiras until the end of the month, but soon learned the particular reason which had prevented our regiment from disembarking at Lisbon.

Chapter 14.

Soult Surprised at Oporto

Sir Arthur Wellesley had landed on the 22nd of April, 1809, at Lisbon, where he was received with every demonstration of joy. On the 24th of the same month, he had joined the army, which up to that period had kept possession of the right bank of the Tagus, and, under the command of General Cradock, had pushed on to Coimbra. From this place, Sir Arthur broke up, on the 7th of May, for the purpose of attacking Oporto, where lay Marshal Soult with the chief of his staff.

On the 15th instant, the agreeable intelligence reached us, at Figueiras, of the deliverance of Oporto, which had been invested on three sides, and the French marshal consequently obliged to make a precipitate escape. A general officer, with 800 men, had, owing to this, been captured by the English; Soult not having at all anticipated the attack, and imagining the British general to be still at Lisbon. Thus taken by surprise, he suffered an inconsiderable English force to effect the passage of the Douro, and did not offer the least molestation until they had crossed that river.

The exultation occasioned at Figueiras by this news was extreme; the bells of all the churches were set in motion, and everybody who could procure such costly articles fell to discharging squibs and crackers. Three, successive nights was the town illuminated, and bonfires glowed in every street. In fact, the worthy Portuguese seemed content to build their whole hopes upon the skill and valour of their heretic allies.

During this interval, I indulged in a survey: of the adjoining country, which exhibits a pleasant diversity of meadow, rock,, and hill. The roads, even to principal cities, are miserably bad, being often left precisely as chance had formed them. No carriage drawn by horses is to be seen; such as are employed, being worked by oxen, mules, or asses.

On the 1st of June, we broke up from Figueiras, in the midst of intense rain, which sadly impeded the rapidity of our progress. Passing through several small places on the road, we were loudly greeted by the natives with "*Viva Inghilterra*," and in many instances flowers were strewn in our path, whilst at one spot a triumphal arch had been erected for the occasion.

After encountering various difficulties, (being at one halting-place unable to procure even straw to rest upon,) we at length struck into the only highroad, properly so called, which Portugal could boast, namely, that which runs from Lisbon, through Leiria and Coimbra, to Oporto. But even this was, at several points, terribly sandy and full of ruts. The country around presented little; other wood than pine-trees. Near Pombal, our attention was arrested by two very picturesque objects;—one, the ruins of a monastery—the other, the remains of a castle which was supposed to have existed in the time of the Moors.

Leiria is a tolerably handsome town, containing several fine churches and elegant houses; but the utter absence of regularity in the disposition of these buildings tends to injure their effect considerably. The streets, like those of Figueiras, are narrow and dirty; but the two market-places, each of which forms a semicircle, display some uniformity and taste.

The town lies in a valley, surrounded by hills, whereon stand other relics of Moorish architecture. Yet, although evidently a place of high consideration, Leiria seemed to swarm, in common with the other Portuguese towns through which I had passed, with mendicants and idlers, who were lounging or lying about on all sides, and appeared to be plunged in the extremity of ignorance and superstition.

In order to avoid utter dependence on the provision made for us by the inhabitants of the country, stores were forwarded from England, consisting of oats, hay, biscuit, and salt beef. In the villages on our line of march, we could get no other but miserable wine, and the whole progress was slow, tedious, and unsatisfactory. On the 6th of June we quitted the high road, and pursued our toilsome course over alternate lofty mountains and sandy plains, or across desolate heaths thinly strewn with pine-trees, sometimes not encountering more than one cottage in the space of five leagues. To add to other inconveniences, we often felt most severely the want of water.

After having crossed the Estrilla range of mountains, which, commencing at Lisbon, traverses the kingdom, and ultimately joins the Pyrenees, we reached the town of Golegan, where we remained until the 14th of June, this being the place appointed for our junction with the main army. Golegan has a greater appearance of regularity than the town last described, but in every other respect it is miserable-looking enough, the houses being destitute of windows, and wearing generally a cheerless and poverty-stricken aspect; but, on entering, the traveller is agreeably surprised to find clean and well-furnished apartments, with vaulted ceilings and gilded cornices.

The heat had by this time increased to an intolerable degree, and thousands of insects, (wasps, flies, &c.) called into a brief existence by the scorching sun, contributed to annoy my outward man both night and day. Altogether, the pretty dreams which I had engendered on ship-board of the luxurious clime of Portugal were fast fleeting away, the occasional clusters of lemon and orange-trees not being sufficient to perpetuate the charm. In fact, we began to rival, in personal appearance, the lean and sallow natives themselves, and even the horses languished and wore an air of dissatisfaction.

A sandy road running from Abrantes to Lisbon passes through Golegan; but it is curious enough that scarce ever was there a traveller to be seen upon it excepting the postboy, whose approach was announced by the smacking of his immensely-long whip. It cannot, to be sure, be matter of surprise that during the hot season the inhabitants of this country should be sparing of exercise, since the slightest motion is sometimes felt to be laborious. Towards evening, however, a cool wind generally starts up, which frequently terminates in a rough breeze.

During our stay in this town, which was prolonged beyond anticipation, we learnt that Sir Arthur Wellesley did not intend to press forward into Spain without having duly weighed the complex circumstances wherein the Peninsula was placed, and concerted some regular system of action with the Spanish generals. The junta of government in that kingdom had found it no easy task to consolidate the various views and opinions of their chiefs. In the month of July, however, an arrangement was entered into with General Cuesta, by virtue whereof the British commander at length decided on crossing the Spanish frontier.

Excursion to Lisbon upon the river Tagus.

On the 14th of June I received orders to go down the Tagus to Lisbon, where a part of our regiment had landed. The river, at our point of starting, did not, in breadth, equal the Weser at its widest part, and in spite of some heavy rain which fell about this period, was exceedingly shallow. In several places we encountered sandbanks and other shoals, whereby our progress was a good deal impeded. The Portuguese boatmen who rowed were too lazy and negligent to make any efforts towards getting the boat along, and in repeated instances we, stuck fast for a good while.

On either bank we met with rising ground, covered with vines, olive-trees, &c. The river shortly, however, widened, and we gradually perceived, in front of us, and on both sides, towns and villages. In the afternoon we arrived at Santarem, having passed five hours most unpleasantly in this small boat. Here we intended to pass the night.

Santarem is a large town lying on a height close to the Tagus, and the paltry-looking coffee-houses, &c. come down to the very water's edge: but, in order to procure a night's lodging, or indeed anything besides coffee, I was compelled to ascend the hill, which was extremely steep, and in places presented huge fissures of the rock.

Hence, it took me full an hour to reach my destined lodging, and even then I was well-nigh obliged to turn back, as I found myself billeted in a house completely empty. Fortunately, however, I met with a good friend belonging to the Legion, who benevolently accommodated me with a share of his quarters. I should have fared very ill but for this:—not having found, since my entering Portugal, any inn bearing the most distant comparison to those of other countries.

Coffee-houses, on the other hand, abound, and the beverage is taken black (without milk) and in large glasses. People who travel generally put up at the houses of relatives and friends; and those who are so unfortunate as to be destitute of either, not uncommonly pass the night under the canopy of heaven.

Next morning we started from Santarem in a vessel of considerable size, and towards midday arrived at Villa Franca, the houses whereof, being built of gray rock-stone, cut a very gloomy-looking figure. The greater part of the town lies on the bank of the river, but a portion of it climbs the mountain behind. Here were several English transport-ships at anchor. Near this place four branches of the Tagus meet, and combine to form a stream of very considerable width and depth.

The course of the river likewise becomes less sinuous, and its shores present many picturesque objects. In fact, taking my view from the middle of the Tagus at this point, I should have considered Portugal as an earthly Paradise, had I not most unfortunately acquired some experience in detail; for the houses on either bank are large and neat in their exterior, and surrounded by well-stocked gardens and vineyards; and even the manufactories which here and there exhibited themselves bore the appearance of palaces.

Wind and tide conspired to favour our passage down the river, and towards five o'clock we found ourselves in the neighbourhood of the capital. Lisbon affords, at some distance, an imposing spectacle, being shaped like an amphitheatre, and situated upon high ground, in order to ascend to the top of which a full hour is occupied: and if we add to the metropolis the suburb of

Belem, a mass of houses is at once presented to the eye stretching (in breadth) over a space of two leagues. The whole scene, in short, would be unexceptionably magnificent, were it not for numerous structures which (owing to the visitations of earthquake) were wretched-looking and ruinous.

A very curious effect arises from the unequal nature of the ground, whence the various streets, &c. (whether dilapidated or in good plight,) towering one above another, induce the stranger, to suppose that the houses are innumerable stories in height; whilst from out the immense mass of buildings, churches, convents, and palaces protrude their lofty crests, and overtop with proud dignity their humbler neighbours.

In the immediate vicinity of Lisbon the Tagus widens so much that its shores almost recede from view: and closer still, it is separated by a high rock, one of its channels proceeding (after several subdivisions) through the province of Alentejo, whilst the other and larger branch washes the foot of the capital.

At various points are broad and high steps, forming landing-places. We sailed slowly as far as the fish-market, the vicinity whereof was characterised by an odour very different from what ought properly to have expanded itself in such a quarter. Our olfactories were indeed most inhospitably invaded, and we thought it peculiarly fortunate that no scrutiny opposed our jumping ashore and quitting the neighbourhood with all possible despatch.

To make progress, however, was no such easy matter, for we had to elbow through a whole swarm of dirty, miserable-looking, ragged, and barefooted scrubs, who pestered us unceasingly with their offers of service. One of the first objects that struck my observation was a multitude of booths, whereat, upon coarse linen, were displayed great varieties of the most tempting. fruit, the evident freshness and beauty of which did not, however, suffice to tickle my appetite, so qualmish had it become from the gales proceeding from the fish-market

I was a good deal puzzled, owing to my ignorance of the language, regarding the course necessary to be pursued in the provision of quarters. I was in good luck, however:—for, whilst. thus doubtful and apprehensive, I at last took heart and addressed a tradesman in French, of whom I inquired after a good inn, and who, to my unspeakable satisfaction, soon turned out to be a fellow-countryman—a glass-merchant from Bohemia. By him I was politely furnished with a guide, who conducted me to a tavern, the landlord of which was a Scot.

Scarcely however had I taken refreshment before I was waited on by several British naval officers, who invited me to attend a ball which was to be given in that same house—an invitation which I accepted principally out of curiosity, and from a natural feeling of surprise at finding myself thus, on a sudden, emerging from uncomfortable solitariness into jovial company. The party proved to consist of various English and Irish families, including the officers of the different British ships then lying at anchor in the Tagus.

In order to transact my business, I had to climb sundry steep and narrow streets, in many instances smelling most offensively, and on descending which, the mud and filth of all descriptions rendered my footing very unsure. To this mass of dirt and foul smells, a most agreeable contrast is afforded the pedestrian who has resolution to attain the very top of the hill,—a point justly denominated "Buenos Ayres," since it not only commands a bewitching prospect, but from its height partakes not of the pestilential atmosphere below, and is, indeed, visited by cool and balmy breezes from the sea.

Amongst other large buildings, a fine hospital stands here, which at the time I speak of was the general receptacle for the English sick. Close by is a royal chapel, and several of the foreign ambassadors reside at this charming spot.

What, however, made this height to me peculiarly delightful, was the sight which is thence commanded of the mouth of the Tagus and of the broad Atlantic into which it empties itself; whilst underneath him, the astonished spectator beholds outstretched the metropolis of Portugal. The mountains which uplift themselves on the other side of the river, and the forts which protect its entrance, combine to increase the general effect. On every side towards the land beautiful gardens are spread; and in the distance the eye encounters that celebrated aqueduct, the middle arch whereof is said to be so lofty as to admit of a line-of-battle ship, in full sail, passing underneath. On the whole, the prospect is one of the most extensive, various, and majestic that the mind can conceive.

On the afternoon of the day whereupon I made the ascent to Buenos Ayres, I wandered through the straight-running streets which lie in the lower part of Lisbon, and the perambulation of which was rendered comparatively pleasant by my previous fatigue. The principal of these, which skirt the river, and consequently are at the foot of the hill, are built regularly enough, particularly such as have been made since the earthquake of 1755: but throughout they are dirty and stinking.

The houses are all colossal in size, massively built, and rising from five to six stories in height. The clumsy, thick pillars, four feet high, which skirt the footpath of the long streets, have an appearance particularly sombre; they are about four feet asunder, and connected by chains which consequently bound the pavement.

These pavements are however only to be met with in the gold and silver streets, the middle space of which is in most instances very badly pitched—in some, not at all; and which streets justly merit their appellation, being chiefly occupied by gold or silversmiths, who expose for sale quantities of valuable goods. From hence, I proceeded to the great King's Square, which comprised three sides of buildings at that time irregular and incomplete. The fourth side has steps leading to the river. In the lower part of the square is a huge archway, under which is situated the Exchange, together with various warehouses and shops.

The colossal statue, on horseback, of King Joseph I. which stands in the centre of this square, and which was erected by that monarch, may perhaps be considered one of the finest specimens of that kind of art in Europe. It is thirty-six feet high; and the immense block of stone which serves as a pedestal rests upon a base six feet from the ground. On one side stand the figures of a man and a tame elephant; upon the other, that of a fiery-looking steed with a man curbing it. This splendid monument is contrasted strangely with several of the surrounding buildings, which are partly in ruins from the effects of earthquake.

From the King's Square, I repaired to the public promenade at the foot of the hill, which is thickly planted with lemon, pine, and cypress trees; but even here, the sweet fragrance of these plants is overpowered by the odour of the adjoining poultry-market, where the fowls are plucked and sold, the feathers, &c. being suffered to accumulate in heaps until devoured by the dogs and swine, or washed away by rain.

Lisbon is not well-lighted; only here and there is a lamp to be seen, notwithstanding the country produces so much oil. There is a general air of life and motion, although the actors on the scene present no very engaging appearance. Beggars, cripples, porters, Moors, and negroes abound. Whole rows of mules, in couples, with jingling bells attached to them, are frequently encountered; and the melody resulting herefrom is agreeably blended with the rumbling of the cart-wheels, (drawn by oxen,) and, occasionally, with the grating of the chains of poor devils of culprits, strung together in parties. To this music, time is beaten by the various venders of goods, who scruple not to chant loud *paeans* in laudation of their different wares; nor must I forget the unceremonious shouts of the porters, demanding clear passage for themselves and loads.

Prepare next, my gentle reader, for a procession of the priesthood, bearing the host, before which every knee must bow, whether Catholic, heretic, or pagan,—whether the ground be dry, wet, or muddy. This kind of thing is common enough; but you will seldom meet, I assure you, with a decent-looking carriage, or a well dressed man;—and still more seldom with a respectable woman.

I remained until the 19th of June in "*Lisboa*,"[1] as the Por-

---

1. This word signifies fair, delightful, and the inhabitants esteem their city (not without some reason as regards its situation) the finest place under the sun.

tuguese call their capital,—though why, God knows! for every inhabitant seems to regard the street as a common sewer, into which he does not hesitate to discharge what, amongst better-mannered people, is concealed from publicity—not thrust upon it. In vain did I (towards night) seek protection from the descending horrors by confining myself to the very middle of the street; for even there the pollution reaches. It is true, the warning note of "*guarda*!" is sometimes given; but, alas! before you are aware from what quarter the evil threatens, it is upon you.

There are two bridges in Lisbon, but not over water; on the contrary, they somewhat resemble aqueducts, as through the arches underneath streets frequently run, wherein you walk whilst horses and carriages are prancing and rolling over your head.

Sunday is not much regarded here. Trade proceeds as usual, nor are the common cries of the town in the least intermitted. The higher classes, it is true, dress rather better than ordinary, and attend mass, where they drop upon their knees, with edifying humility, side-by-side with the low-born and ragged.

Chapter 15

Return up the Tagus

At eleven o'clock, p. m. of the 19th of June, I started from Lisbon, on my return to the regiment, in company with several other officers. This voyage was by no means agreeable. I had, indeed, before I set out, been given to understand that the stream would be against us,—that the passage would, consequently, be extremely tedious,—and that I should be unable to come up with my regiment until it had penetrated deep into Spain. But I did not anticipate the difficulty which I found, even in procuring a boat from the proper authorities. It was midnight when the tide served; and I had to prepare for passing the night in an open boat, with the extra advantage of rain, which had just set in.

Early in the morning, we reached Villa Franca, where we breakfasted; and towards nightfall, (having made no more than a couple of leagues in the mean time, from want of wind,) our boatmen very coolly fastened the boat to the shore, and, after frying and eating some fish, which they had brought with them, deliberately composed themselves to sleep! I had likewise provided some refreshment, and it was well that I had, since there was no inhabited place in the neighbourhood.

The fine moonlight rendered my dreary situation more tolerable; but, as morning approached, I was roused from slumber by a swarm of mosquitoes, to get rid of which, I speedily plunged into the Tagus. Having taken my bathe, I stirred up the snoring boatmen, upon whose well-seasoned carcasses the attacks of the mosquitoes were innocuous; and, although with no great alacrity, they proceeded to push off the boat in good earnest.

At the *Tajo Novo,* (as a particular part of the stream is denominated,) we exchanged our heavy boat for a lesser one; all which latter description of vessels were detained, by means of an English force stationed here for the purpose. It is true, some unreasonable people objected to exchange their property for articles less commodious; whereupon the British soldiers (in order to inculcate more liberal principles) brought them to by a salute of musketry.

On our arrival, we found sundry heavy barges, laden with money and provisions for the army, awaiting at this place the seizure of lighter craft; and I therefore anticipated a vexatious delay, perhaps of several days. In this prospect, we got cabins erected on the shore, to shield us from the excessive heat by day, and from the abominable mosquitoes by night. Fortunately, an English officer of the commissariat was on the spot, through whose friendly intervention we procured fresh provisions, whereof we lost no time in availing ourselves.

Next morning, the politeness of the resident English officer supplied us with a convenient boat, which carried us on rather more pleasantly; and, on the approach of evening, having made fast our bark, we sallied forth to a village hard by, to purchase provisions. Here I was astonished by a spectacle of a most extraordinary nature; in various parts of the village, large bonfires had been lighted; and on advancing nearer, I distinguished a number of grotesque figures, in a state of perfect nudity, skipping with all sorts of antic gestures around and over the flames.

By the strange and somewhat ghastly light, the bodies of these fantastic revellers appeared almost black; and, as they attempted to outvie each other in leaping across the blaze, I half-questioned my waking faculties, and had a strong persuasion that I must be dreaming of some savage tribe of Indians. We made up to them, however; and soon found that this, so far from being any pagan rite, was the celebration of the Christian festival of St. John! I was immediately hailed and environed by a strong party of these free and easy gentry, to whose unsophisticated perceptions I was an object of great curiosity. I found them, however, civil enough, and extremely ready to furnish me (for a proper consideration) with eggs, wherewith (not feeling any particular confidence in my company) I decamped off hand.

The heat on the following morning was intolerable; added to which, we were wholly deserted by the wind. Towards evening, however, it freshened a little, but not to much purpose, and ultimately we were obliged to lay-to in a spot where there was neither tree nor cottage. Under these desolate circumstances, I had no choice but to take a drink of Tagus water, and stretch myself in the boat to sleep, with as much complacency as I could assume.

On awaking, I found, to my utter surprise, that our boatmen had taken themselves off, having been smitten with a devotional fit, which led them to attend mass at the nearest church,—the festival of St. John being still in course. Although this line of proceeding was doubtless highly laudable, yet I must confess I should have been more edified thereby had they chosen for the occasion a less ill-timed period; and as matters stood, not relishing any longer abstinence from food! I despatched a couple of hussars, to use some gentle military persuasion, whereby I doubted not they would perceive the propriety of returning for the present to their temporal duties, and am happy to say my style of argument proved convincing. In fact, despatch was now become indispensable; we were most anxious to come up with our regiment, which had already gained the Spanish frontier; and besides this, our pecuniary supply was rapidly decreasing.

On the afternoon of this day, we reached the point whereat I had embarked, on my passage down the river; and finding no troops there, proceeded on to Barquinha, where lay two battalions of the legion, amongst whom I met with several old friends, and in their society cast aside all my former chagrin.

On the 4th of July, after a long and tedious march, I reached Castel Branco, a fortified place on the Portuguese frontier, and here I unexpectedly met with a division of our regiment, and once more vaulted with alacrity into my saddle. The main body of the regiment was already in Spain, but this battalion had for the most part been quartered in a dilapidated country-house, of which the major had taken possession; and with him I established myself.

On the 6th inst. we broke up quarters, and pursued our march through an uninteresting dreary country, presenting nothing but rocks, stunted trees, and barren heaths. At Lodoira, a mean dirty place, we passed the night; and the following day proceeded to Zebreira, the country about which was of an equally unpromising aspect, but flatter, and the town itself more considerable in point of size.

The nearer we approached to Spain, the more poverty-stricken did the people look. In Zebreira, children up to ten or twelve years of age, frisked about quite naked, whilst their parents were covered with rags. The main articles of food used by these poor creatures seemed to be cabbages and Turkish wheat.

Chapter 16

Sickness Among the Troops

On the 8th of July, 1809, we entered upon the Spanish territory, passing by Salvatierra, and on to Sarsa Lamayor. The two kingdoms are at this point separated by the small river Elvas, which at that time of year had so little water that we could without difficulty ride across it. Sarsa Lamayor is a pretty large town, the houses of which present a somewhat better aspect than ordinary: but we could not succeed in procuring as good a supply of provisions as was desirable. Bread, wine, and cheese made of goat's milk, formed the only provender which money could command.

We were obliged to pass two days here, in order to await the joining of the paymaster. The Sabbath is observed with greater decorum than in Portugal; and the inhabitants (as in most frontier towns) understand, although they do not commonly speak, the language of the adjoining country. The Spanish villages are not so inaccessible in their situation as those it was my lot to visit in Portugal, and they are more cleanly and built with a greater attention to comfort. This favourable comparison cannot, however, be extended to the inhabitants, who are proud and unconciliatory.

Our speculations as to the ground possible to be got over *per diem* were frustrated by the precipitate shutting-in of evening; even in the midst of summer, the sun goes down in this latitude at half-past seven, and night quickly ensues, much darker than at the corresponding season in Germany.

In a few days' time, however, we at length overtook the main body of our regiment, which, together with the rest of the English army, was bivouacking under olive-trees, in the neighbourhood of Placentia, whereat head-quarters were established. The object in stopping here was to give opportunity for the junction of several regiments not yet come up, and to await the arrival of transports with provisions and ammunition.

The heat was at this point of time so intense that the fat of bacon, even when placed in the shade, speedily dissolved; and metallic substances of various kinds, such as swords, buttons, &c. having been a short time exposed to the rays of the sun, blistered the finger which should presume to handle them! Yet, strangely enough, even at the moment of profuse perspiration my skin was to the touch icy cold. Our covering and couches by night were composed of our cloaks and the housings of our horses, as the army was unprovided with tents, and the straw in Spain is not calculated to lie on, being trodden down by the oxen.

Placentia, the chief city of Estremadura, bears few marks of the capital of a province, and is surrounded by very bad roads. The bridge which runs across the Xerte, as well as the walls encompassing the town, (which are said to be of Moorish construction,) are in a very dilapidated condition; the streets are narrow—the houses high and ill-looking. The churches and convents (of which there are a great number) form the chief—indeed, almost the only ornaments of the place. The latter now answered the purpose of military hospitals. On the top of the principal church, a number of storks had taken up their quarters. In one of the monasteries near this city the Emperor Charles V. terminated his restless life.

We were now on the eve of participating in great events. Joseph Bonaparte, with the garrison of Madrid, the guard, and the corps under General Sebastiani, (in all 25,000 men,) was encamped in the vicinity of the metropolis; and Marshal Victor, with 85,000 men, lay at Talavera de la Reina, on the banks of the Tagus and the Alberche. Against these several forces, which subsequently effected a junction, the English army marched, having united itself with a Spanish force amounting to 35,000 men, commanded by General Cuesta, and both armies appeared resolved to come to a general engagement.

On the afternoon of the 16th of July, our hussar regiment, in common with the rest of the British cavalry, was for the first time reviewed by Sir Arthur Wellesley: and on the following day, the troops broke up into several columns, and proceeded forthwith to join General Cuesta.

On the 23rd, we found ourselves in the neighbourhood of Talavera, and preparations were made at ten o'clock a. m. to attack the enemy in his strong-hold the other side of the Alberche. These preparations, however, turned out to be useless; the Spanish general declining the honour of taking his share, in consequence, as some said, of its being the Sabbath.[1] Meanwhile, the French troops were situated so close to us that their huts were plainly to be descried. After a few hours of inactivity, we fell back again upon our former position, where we had bivouacked the preceding night. This was a favourable opportunity lost of combating the foe while he was single-handed; and thus was time afforded to Victor for retreating quietly, and achieving his junction with Joseph and Sebastiani, by which means the hostile army was swollen to between 50,000 and 60,000 men.

On the 24th of July, at three a. m. we once more broke up, in order to attack the enemy. We were now all united, and in full expectation of the event. On we marched, no drum or trumpet sounding, in impressive silence broken only by the measured tramp of the advancing corps. We halted in a wood on the bank of the Alberche, and here soon learnt from our piquets that the hostile troops were fled! We afterwards understood that they had retired upon Santa Olalla, where they anticipated meeting with Sebastiani.

---

1. This disinclination, and the reason advanced, savours more of the ecclesiastic than of the soldier. General Cuesta would have been wiser had he remembered that one of Napoleon's armies lay before him; by whom such pious distinctions would be utterly disregarded. In fact, the French Emperor derived considerable advantage from his total neglect of similar scruples, and would no doubt have laughed heartily at the Spaniard's tender conscience.

Our brigade of light cavalry and a division of infantry under General Sherbrooke, proceeded to pass through the river, whereby the latter were obliged to wade up to their middle; and having gained the opposite bank, took possession of Victor's abandoned encampment, which was formed of huts constructed of boards, branches of trees, earth, &c. On advancing a league further, we found several dead bodies scattered about, and prisoners were every now and then sent in by the piquets.

We marched three leagues on to Cassalegos, where the horrors of a seat of war were painfully conspicuous. The town was quite deserted and for the most part ruinous;—our bivouac was in a corn-field, which had been so trodden down by the enemy as to yield little worth having even as provender for the horses. In fact, we found, generally speaking, that the privations and difficulties of a soldier's life are greatly augmented in southern climates.

The common want of water is most distressingly felt, particularly as the eyes get blinded with thick dust, to remove which that refreshing liquid is indispensable. Our nights were spent upon the bare ground, and seldom had we opportunity of prolonging our slumbers beyond three hours. Hence, our bodies grew black from the effects of the dust, and attenuated from the relaxing heat; and to such a degree did this metamorphosis extend, that very frequently the most intimate friends could not recognise each other. After their slight and unrefreshing sleep, the countenances of the men, even on beginning their daily march, looked wan and feverish: and under these circumstances, it was not surprising that the hospitals soon became overstocked.

On the 25th of July, we remained lying near Cassalegos; and our advanced guard, which had pushed as far as Santa Olalla, returned. Various unpleasant rumours now got afloat; among the rest, it was said that Sir Arthur Wellesley had reason to complain of the backwardness of the Spanish Junta in making good their engagements with regard to furnishing the proper supplies, on which account he found it prudent to check his advance until the affair should be satisfactorily arranged. Hence, only two brigades of infantry and one of cavalry had been sent across the river, the main army remaining near, and the head quarters in, Talavera.

General Cuesta, however, notwithstanding these obstacles, proceeded onward with his army and penetrated as far as Santa Olalla, pushing his advanced guard to Torrijos, whilst the English troops did not push beyond Santa Olalla, where they established themselves, to keep open the communication with the Spaniards as well as with the Lusitanian Legion, commanded by General Wilson, stationed in Escalona.

The Spanish general, Venagas not having however, according to agreement, interposed to frustrate the junction of Victor, Sebastiani, and Joseph, but remained at Daymiel, in La Mancha, (according, as it was said, to orders he had received from the Junta,) the consequence was that the combined French army attacked Cuesta on the 26th, near Torrijos, and, as we were informed by our piquets, succeeded in driving him back. The truth of this intelligence was indeed soon rendered manifest by the arrival of the Spaniards, at first singly but soon in large bodies, and in evident confusion, and it became obvious that the enemy might almost immediately be expected by ourselves.

Hence, we found it necessary to break up from Cassalegos, at three o'clock on the morning of the 27th; and the division of infantry, with the brigade of light cavalry, formed itself in battle array on the road to Madrid. After awaiting the enemy in vain for the space of several hours, we returned to our bivouac, and the men had scarcely dismounted and made preparations for breakfast, before the approaching thunder of cannon and the summons "to arms!" sent them again into their saddles.

Within ten minutes the line of battle was once more formed. The enemy were at this moment engaged with our advanced guard, and their balls reached our position. As, according to Sir Arthur Wellesley's plan of action, no resistance was to be offered at this point, if it could possibly be avoided, the infantry slowly retreated with as much order as if on parade, and their retreat was covered by the cavalry.

Towards two o'clock in the afternoon, we reached the Alberche, the enemy still at our heels and continually skirmishing with our rear, though without occasioning the slightest confusion. We crossed the stream in the utmost regularity, having set fire to the huts which had been left by the enemy, the flames from this dry wood mounting high into the still air, and communicating conflagration to the surrounding corn-fields. In this manner was an immense plain, which might have accommodated 20,000 men, filled with smoke, obscuring the heavens, and presenting an aspect of gloomy horror. On our side of the river, several pieces of artillery had been planted, which, as soon as our troops had passed it, kept up an unceasing fire upon the pursuers.

In the evening we arrived near Talavera, the position which had been selected by Sir Arthur Wellesley as a rallying point; but before we had reached it, a body of French which had forded the river at a point higher up attacked one of our divisions of infantry and the rear-guard of our cavalry, in which affair General Mackenzie and several other officers were killed.

The British troops, in this instance, had hardly time to form, still less to occupy the ground designed for them, owing to the precipitate assault of the enemy. The cannonading was heavy, and our Spanish friends not liking its probable results, made no scruple to get away as they could, imagining themselves unsafe even within the entrenchments. The mules which bore our baggage had got into disorder, and the highway was consequently so blocked up by them and the artillery that we were obliged to cut paths through lanes and vineyards to the appointed position, which was stony and mountainous.

Here we shared a repast of bread and wine, acceptable enough to me who had lived all the previous part of the day merely on dry chocolate and water. Up to a very late hour, wounded soldiers and stray baggage-wagons were brought in, and the former complained bitterly of the Spanish brigands, who seemed to prefer spoiling the English to fighting the French.

Chapter 17

Battle of Talavera

The morning of the eventful 28th July, 1809, dawned upon the rough and broken slumbers of our host, and was ushered in by a tremendous discharge of cannon and musketry. Our horses had been kept through the whole night saddled and bridled, and we had but to leap upon their backs. A stone had been my pillow, and a mantle my covering.

Having taken up our ground, we found our brigade situated on the left wing of the army; to the right of us was the town of Talavera; to the left, a high hill; and in front, several hillocks, which served to cover our position. The other cavalry brigades took their ground, as they rode up, more towards the centre of the main army. The entire position, which had been selected by the quick glance of the British commander-in-chief, might have extended a league in breadth.

The centre of the army, under General Campbell, was planted on a rising ground, in front of which entrenchments had been thrown up a day or two before; its left, commanded by General Hill, occupied the rocky heights alluded to; and the right leaned towards the river Tagus. On this side the Spanish troops were stationed, as well as upon the bridge over the Alberche, on the road to Madrid. Immediately in front of the town their force was strongest, forming two lines, which were covered by entrenchments and clumps of olive trees.

On the preceding evening, the enemy, after he had driven back General Mackenzie's division, had succeeded in dislodging

General Hill from his heights; but for a few minutes only, the general's division recovering its ground at the point of the bayonet. In the course of the night, renewed attempts were made by the French to gain possession of this post, but they were in every instance repulsed with great loss. The last of these attacks happened towards morning; and being of a more desperate nature than the. preceding ones, had aroused us from our brief repose.

Towards eight o'clock, the assault upon the British line became general. It was of the most formidable description, but wholly unsuccessful. At eleven, the enemy furiously attacked the right of our army, where the Spaniards were chiefly posted; but on this occasion our allies seemed to rally their energies, and really fought nobly; nor could their opponents gain one inch of advantage.

But throughout the day General Hill's post was the most important, and the most fiercely disputed. During the night, it had been strongly fortified with cannon, and it was here that Sir Arthur Wellesley himself was chiefly to be seen whilst the battle raged. I had opportunities of riding along the entire line, and consequently of observing every circumstance of interest connected with this great conflict.

The almost suffocating heat occasioned the fire to relax a little in the afternoon; about two o'clock, the French made another tremendous attack, in the midst of which, a powder-magazine, near to our brigade, blew up with a frightful explosion, and at the same moment, strong columns of the enemy pushed forward towards the eminence upon which Sir Arthur Wellesley had posted himself.

He immediately despatched an *aide-de-camp* to the light cavalry brigade, with orders to advance directly upon the French position; and it was curious to observe with what despatch the men vaulted into their saddles, having previously been unengaged and merely lookers-on. The horses, many of them, soon wandered back once more disencumbered of their riders, but from a very different cause.

A deep ditch, which ran along in front of the French line,

proved no small obstacle to our assailing regiments; and several brave fellows, in their impetuosity, got dismounted therein. Notwithstanding this drawback, however, the enemy was, by this counter-movement, completely foiled in his purpose of storming the height, and his cavalry put to flight in the greatest disorder; whereby the fire of our artillery was brought to bear upon his infantry-masses with good effect.

Immediately afterwards, our heavy cavalry received instruction to press forward with the Spanish artillery, upon the rear of the French position; and when arrived sufficiently near it, they opened to the right and left, and unmasked a cannonade of murderous severity on the crowded columns of the enemy.

This attack, on our part, was returned by the enemy in an assault on our centre, which was, however, so effectually resisted by the division of General Campbell, supported by a part of the Spanish cavalry, that the assailants left their artillery in our hands. Towards the approach of evening followed the last and most violent attack against the left wing of the centre, under General Sherbrooke, but which was defeated by the firmness and courage of the English guards and the battalions of the German legion, at the point of the bayonet.

In these several movements and contests both sides suffered greatly, the more so as nothing could exceed the ardour of the soldiers. They performed, indeed, prodigies of valour; and in the last assault it was evident that the entire French army had combined; they relished their reception, however, so badly, that, in the course of the night, they retreated altogether across the Alberche.

Late in the evening, our brigade, which had been considerably shorn of its numbers, was directed to fall back into a cornfield at some distance from the field of battle, which had hitherto remained inviolate, and which our hungry horses fell upon like wolves. The wounded were removed to Talavera; and thus ended this important day, the result of which spread the greatest consternation amongst the French troops, who were, it seems; rather inclined to undervalue either the skill or the prowess (or perhaps both) of the allies. Joseph Bonaparte, seeing Madrid threatened by General Venagas, who was in its neighbourhood with a considerable force, gave orders to Sebastiani to march against him, whilst Victor was obliged to retreat back to Santa Olalla.

On the morning of the 29th instant, part of our hussar regiment received orders to proceed across the field of battle, to the banks of the Alberche, and there to form a chain of oat-posts, as the army found itself too weak to pursue its advantage in good earnest; for although a division of fresh troops under General Crawford, which had recently disembarked from Ireland, had joined us the same morning on the ground, they were equally incapacitated from fatigue, as we from the losses and exhaustion of the combat; since, for the purpose of taking part in the battle, they had accomplished nearly sixty miles within the last twenty-four hours. As the victory was already gained, these newcomers. were used towards strengthening the line of outposts.

Several days had now elapsed since I had taken any warm nourishment. These matters one is careless about in a state of warfare; but, this morning I found myself strongly tempted to regale upon a dish of chocolate, and accordingly (the servants being all with the baggage-wagons) proceeded to cook some in an empty cartridge-box,—the materials for my fire consisting of sundry handsomely gilt looking-glass frames! Having despatched this dainty meal, I rode off to overtake my comrades in their progress to the Alberche.

The field of battle presented a spectacle truly dreadful! A space extending several leagues was almost literally covered with the slain! On the fatal height which had been so gallantly disputed, our courageous fellows lay as if they had been entire battalions taking their natural rest—painfully conspicuous from the red uniform; whilst, within fifty paces, clad in blue and grey, were heaped in dense masses the bodies of the assailants! Amongst the latter, many, who were wounded only, called out to us for succour, which we were completely unable to extend.

All the brushwood, trees, cottages, &c. in the vicinity, were reduced to ashes, and the earth itself looked black and blasted:—

whilst, added to this universal desolation, the scorching rays of the sun contributed their influence to increase the torments of the unfortunate wounded wretches. Amidst the many thousand dead bodies, brute animals, likewise, were mingled. Arms, broken carriages, powder-wagons, chests,—in short, a heterogeneous medley, comprising all manner of articles, was scattered about, to complete this picture of destruction and woe.

The very bushes, half-burnt, were in many instances clogged with dead bodies, both human and brute—unhappy creatures who had crawled thither, wounded, from the scene of strife, and been finished by the fiery masses wherefrom their exhaustion prevented escape. Thus the devastating principle of fire lent aid to the great work of slaughter; nor was the ministry of the demons of hunger and thirst wanting:—on approaching the Alberche, some poor wretches were discovered by our men who had lain there since the 27th instant, and whose parched lips had not, they said, been blessed with a drop of water during the two days' interval.

We bivouacked under some oaktrees which had remained unscathed, and a neighbouring cornfield also did us much service. A medicine-chest that had been abandoned by the enemy was brought in, and supplied us with many articles whereof we stood in great need. Our *vedettes* were posted on one ride the river and those of the enemy on the other.

On the following day, the wounded (both friends and foes) were conveyed slowly, upon carts drawn by oxen, to the hospital, and several battalions were ordered to accomplish the interment of the dead. A number of our wounded who had unluckily fallen into the hands of the enemy and had suffered much maltreatment, now arrived (on being discarded to shift for themselves) at our bivouac.

An English officer who was among them exhibited a picture of the utmost human misery! A ragged Spanish peasant led the faint and panting horse whereupon this unfortunate soldier rather hung than sate: he was wounded in the head and foot, and his wounds were well nigh bare, and bleeding fast. His uniform, owing to the gold lace having been torn away, was thoroughly defaced, and he was destitute at once of hat, shoes, and stockings—the only covering for his legs being a pair of large worn-out Spanish boots.

Upon his countenance sate despair, and the cravings of hunger and thirst were likewise depicted in its lines. With a sensation of deep interest did we behold the transient smile which spread over his wan features on once more beholding his companions in arms—who, however, were unable to afford him any other refreshment than their consolation and a drink of fresh water.

That sleep is the chief necessary of human existence, and goes in its effects far beyond the administering to hunger or thirst, I had a convincing proof in the course of the night of the 30th July. During the previous three days and nights I had scarcely enjoyed as many hours' sleep: besides which, I had been necessitated to put up frequently with but a little bread, wine, and chocolate—and often with none of these, but water only.

At length provisions arrived, but were not to be served out till midnight. I had previously composed myself upon a delicious bundle of straw, and slept most sweetly! On awaking in the morning, much refreshed, I could not avoid expressing to an officer who lay beside me my regret at not having aroused myself to partake of the meat and soup.

After listening awhile to my doleful lamentations, he excited in me no small surprise by saying that I had so partaken,—had been awakened—devoured my share with uncommon complacency—and dropped off to sleep again; and in a few moments the whole circumstance floated dimly upon my recollection, like a dream.

The loss of the allies during these three days (namely the 26th, 27th, and 28th) amounted to 10,000 men in killed, wounded, and prisoners; of which number about 5000 English and 3000 Spanish fell on the latter or great day of the battle. The French loss amounted to about 12,000 men, twenty cannon, and numerous ammunition-wagons.

On the 1st of August we were relieved by another battalion

of our regiment; and as the enemy had, during the preceding night, abandoned his position on the opposite bank of the Alberche, a detachment was sent in pursuit of him, which found that he had fallen back as far as Santa Olalla. In Cassalegos he had left behind him a number of badly-wounded men.

On marching back, to rejoin the main body of the army, our course led us over the ground which had been occupied by the Spaniards, and here the scene of slaughter was terrific; whilst, owing to the intolerable heat, the dead bodies had already become putrefied, and exhaled a stench absolutely pestilential. A well in front of the town, which had hitherto supplied a cool and refreshening liquid, was now literally choked with animal masses fast advancing in decomposition. Our comrades we found stationed close under the walls of Talavera, overshadowed by branching olives. Here we took some soup—abundantly (though not quite so agreeably) seasoned by the clouds of dust which the horses raised as they were driven to an adjacent watering-place.

Talavera de la Reina might in former times have been, possibly, a pleasant town, as it lies on a most fruitful plain irrigated by the Tagus; but at this juncture it presented a very mournful aspect. There lay in the place from 8,000 to 10,000 wounded soldiers of various nations; and the houses, churches, and convents were all in a completely ruinous state and deserted by their proper inhabitants. I had much trouble to procure a decent lodging, although the place takes rank among the largest towns of the kingdom; and it was extremely painful to encounter at every step the supplications of poor wretches to whom one had no power of extending assistance.

The next night (after a lapse of several weeks, during which I slept under the bare sky) I once more occupied a bedchamber, but the close air thereof, combined with the annoyance of troops of insects, effectually prevented my repose and rendered the exchange a positive evil.

Chapter 18

Unexpected Retreat of the Allies

The morning which succeeded this unpleasant night I visited an hospital (which had been established in a convent). In this place I became acquainted with an event which, at first sight, appeared incredible. I found sundry wounded officers in earnest conference over a map of the Peninsula, and pointing out with melancholy interest the prejudicial consequences likely to ensue from this event. No-one could have calculated that the victorious Wellesley (whom the battle just fought was the occasion of elevating to the English peerage under the title of Viscount Wellington) should think it prudent to relinquish his successes, commence a retreat, and abandon a portion of his very wounded to fall into the hands of the conquered enemy.

The news, however, soon proved too true; and if in the morning it were doubted, its certainty became apparent in the afternoon,—when orders were issued that all the sick and wounded (who were not incapable of removal) should be removed in wagons and carts, and the rest, under the care of a commissariat and a body of surgeons, remain in Talavera. This intelligence spread with inconceivable rapidity, and with all sorts of exaggeration, throughout the hospitals: it was said that the defeated foe again advanced from Santa Olalla, and in fact was already on the banks of the Alberche, whilst Marshal Soult pressed upon our rear, in the direction of Placentia.

Hence ensued the utmost consternation and tumult in the streets. Imagination was busy in placing before the wounded all manner of gloomy presages; and those appointed to attend on them ran to and fro, uncertain what measures to take, whilst the patients (both friends and foes) suffered neglect even in the necessary attentions of dressing and bandaging.

Sundry poor devils who had previously thought themselves, and been considered by others, incapable of motion, managed to crawl out of their wards, smitten with the overpowering horror of falling under the "tender mercies" of the French. Any chance was preferred to this: and in a short period the various hospitals were almost empty,—the senior physicians and surgeons being no more desirous of keeping their posts than the poor fellows upon whom they exercised their skill.

The English army had proceeded to Oropesa, whither I (in company with a military chaplain and some wounded officers) followed. We were constantly encountering, on the road, wagons laden with wounded, after which limped a train of miserable objects scarcely able to drag their bodies forward: added to the horrors of war, were the apprehensions necessarily entertained of the Spanish brigands, who were (in common with the peasantry) constantly on the alert to rifle such English soldiers as were led by sickness or fatigue to straggle from their respective corps. Thus, when night came, we took watch by turns whilst our party bivouacked beneath a range of trees.

It was some days before the enigma presented by the existing state of things cleared itself up: but we at length understood the following circumstances:—Lord Wellington had come to an agreement with General Cuesta, on entering Spain, that the passes of Puerto de Banos and Puerto de Penales should be defended by the Spaniards; the first by the Marquess de la Reyna and the other by the Duke del Parque.

The importance of the latter position had induced his Lordship to instruct Marshal Beresford to keep a watchful eye thereupon with the Portuguese force commanded by him, conceiving the former pass to be secure; but on the second day after the battle of Talavera, information was received at head-quarters that Ney and Soult were in full march in our rear towards Puerto de Banos, whilst our flanks were threatened by divisions under Mortier and Victor.

The united forces thus opposed to us were estimated at 60,000 men. General Cuesta was equally anxious to retain possession of Puerto de Banos, and proposed to the commander-in-chief that he should detach General Wilson's corps to its defence. General Wilson himself was present at Talavera; but his division lay in the mountains of Escalona, where his outposts had spread themselves five leagues on the road to Madrid, had actually opened communications within that capital, and performed sundry other important services; in consequence whereof his Lordship could not decide on calling it away.

He therefore suggested to Cuesta the propriety of despatching thither another Spanish corps; but although the latter could not but perceive the peculiar value of Wilson's force, situated as it was, yet he continued averse to detaching any portion of his own army. On the 30th, Lord Wellington's suggestion assumed the shape of a command, which however was still unavailing, until on the 2nd of August news arrived of the positive entrance of the French into Bejar, whereupon General Bassecourt was, at length, detached with a Spanish force, but (as might easily have been anticipated) he arrived too late, the pass being already carried. In fact, the Marquess de la Reyna had (with his inefficient corps) offered little or no resistance, and had retired, by way of Placentia, upon the bridge of Almarez, which he intended to break down behind him.

Cuesta now proposed a separation of the main army,—one-half of it to march upon the enemy's flank, and the other to occupy the position of Talavera. To this arrangement, the English General decidedly objected; saying at the same time that he was ready either to defend the position of Talavera, with the whole British army, or to advance against the enemy in an equally concentrated state. On this, Cuesta expressed a wish that the choice should remain with Lord Wellington, who accordingly determined on marching, and leaving Cuesta in possession of Talavera, to which that general apparently consented. Meantime, however, according to the information obtained on the 1st of August of the enemy's movements, it seemed that, having been foiled in the attempt to possess himself of Talavera, he was disposed to effect a junction with the French army at Placentia, by way of Escalona.

This supposition was confirmed on the 2nd inst. by General Wilson, and Lord Wellington was consequently compelled to adopt decisive measures. He issued peremptory commands to the Spanish general, O'Donoughue to provide without delay a sufficient number of wagons, &c. to remove the sick and wounded from Talavera; as it was not improbable that the French army would press forward (across Escalona) and force Cuesta to abandon that town before the English commander could advance to his succour.

Such was the state of affairs when Lord Wellington broke up from his position and took the road to Oropesa, in order, if possible, to come upon the rear of the hostile army under Soult and Ney, in which movement he was very soon followed (to his surprise and chagrin) by the Spanish general, who appeared to be conscious of no safety, except under the wing of the English army.

After passing the night as I have stated, unacquainted at that time with the delicate situation wherein our leader was involved, we quitted our sylvan encampment by dawn of day, and pursued our route to Oropesa, without even the refreshment of a drink of water, and incomplete ignorance of the road. The reader will therefore judge how great was our satisfaction on finding, in that town, a couple of officers belonging to our regiment, who had been some days there, and in whose cool pleasant quarters we were regaled with a cup of excellent coffee.

They subsequently joined our small squadron, and we continued our progress. We overtook the main force, under arms, at a small village in the vicinity, where they had been two nights and two days, destitute of provisions, awaiting every moment an attack from the *corps d'armée* of Soult and Ney. A corps of observation was now formed, consisting of artillery and light cavalry, and despatched in the direction of the enemy; whilst the remaining part of the cavalry were directed to follow the infantry, which had been put in motion some hours before.

After a march of two leagues, during which we suffered immensely. from heat, we arrived at Fuente-del-Arzobispo, a little hamlet deserted by its inhabitants, situated on the right bank of the Tagus. Close by is a bridge, which crosses this stream, and has two high towers upon it. It is sixty feet long, but very narrow, so that no two carriages could pass over abreast; and as the cavalry was to wait until the infantry had crossed, I, meanwhile, had leisure to find myself desperately hungry, whereat the "candid reader" will not, perhaps, feel surprised, when I tell him, that I had tasted no solid food whatever for the last two days. Hence I was induced to ransack the village in question throughout; but, alas! the inhabitants had not only taken themselves off, but had carefully removed everything in the shape of provender,

The passage of the bridge displayed a very picturesque spectacle. It was precipitantly high, and the various groups which successively crossed it, mingled strangely with each other. English, German, and Spanish troops—men under arms and squadrons of wounded—cavalry and foot-soldiers —baggage-wagons and artillery—combined to create a confusion and uproar scarcely conceivable, and carried on from eight o'clock a. m. until a late hour in the afternoon. On the other side, we came up with the rear of the wounded, who had been forwarded from Talavera, in which place, it appeared that about 1500 had been left behind, whom Lord Wellington commended in a letter to the humane care of Marshal Mortier, nor was his recommendation unavailing.

The passage of the bridge being effected, we had still four leagues to march to our bivouac. Here we were, at length, fortunate enough to receive some bread; this, together with a little ham, (for which I paid extravagantly,) and a draught of Tagus water, formed my nourishment for the day. Fatigued with the long march, and faint from privation of sleep, I threw myself upon my hard couch under an oak-tree; and soon slumbered so soundly, that the residue of bread, (to me a treasure!) which I had placed beside me, had utterly vanished before I awoke. This was, in fact, no small loss; for during the next two days, nothing whatever was served out, and the rigours of famine seemed about to succeed to the dangers of warfare.

On the 5th of August, oppressed with heat and dust, we proceeded four leagues through a desert country, and afterwards bivouacked amidst bramble-bushes, near a small hamlet. The little river Gualega afforded to man and beast the refreshment of water. Hungry and tired, I laid myself down to seek a brief respite from the annoyances inseparable from a military life.

On the following morning we broke up, many of us bearing rather rough intimations of the thorny nature of our lodgement. In this inhospitable tract, no vestige of a tree was to be met with; and thus our worn and weary bodies were perfectly exposed to the unremitting fervour of the burning sun. The greater part of the cavalry dismounted, on any occasion of a halt, and sought refuge for awhile in the narrow shade cast by the figures of the horses. On reaching the mountainous region before us, we were lucky enough to find water for our thirsty steeds.[1]

As evening drew on, the road across these heights became more practicable; and we passed through two deserted villages, neither of which presented any temptation to induce us to stop; we, therefore, held on our course over dreadful roads, and with empty stomachs. The mountains grew loftier and steeper: the cannons were dragged up singly by many horses and men, of which former several sank exhausted upon the road.

About nine o'clock, we came to a halt in the neighbourhood of the village of Torrecillas, and here some flour was divided among the troops. Our march was perpetuated through the dark night, along narrow defiles bordering gigantic precipices, and

---

1. An officer of our regiment, whose good spirits never forsook him, on this occasion caused the trumpet-signal to be given, the sound whereof had so often called us to a cheerful and abundant meal! Upon hearing it, I hurried to him, exclaiming, that as he had invited guests, he could do no less than entertain them: whereupon this kind-hearted man immediately forced on me his last piece of ham, to which another friend added a slice of bread.

admitting only one passenger abreast—so hilly, likewise, either mounting or descending, as to occasion great hazard, on the part of the riders, of slipping into the gulf below. By one o'clock, we reached the spot selected for our bivouac, where, on account of the absence of trees, it was difficult to secure our horses. This day the army had travelled upwards of seven leagues.

Upon this height, the temperature of the atmosphere was almost as severely cold, as that of the plain had been fiercely hot; and to guard against the sudden change, I was obliged to use the utmost precaution. As to the nourishment of food, it was quite out of the question! A comrade, indeed, kindly accommodated me with a cup of chocolate; having taken which, I crept under my rude covering, and really enjoyed a far better night's rest than the circumstances warranted me in expecting.

The numberless cooking-fires kindled by the infantry, the flames whereof crept up the sides of the opposite hill, threw a kind of witchful glare over the otherwise black atmosphere, and rendered the whole scene at once imposing and unearthly. A herd of swine had fallen into the hands of the troops on the preceding day, and their remains were now voraciously swallowed. The system of slaughtering these luckless beasts was simple and expeditious; the bayonet was the instrument of their death, and the limbs were separated by those weapons wherewith nature has provided man.

At six o'clock on the 7th of August, we aroused from our mountain-lair, and beheld with a shuddering sensation the precipitous tracks which had been before shrouded from us by night, and along which lay our farther course. The carcases of horses, and mules strewed the footway, and the broken wheels of various kinds of carriages and pieces of ammunition were scattered profusely here and there, and in no few instances rattled into the chasms below.

As midday advanced, we reached the highest ridge of these mountains, and the vicinity of Truxillo. It was here freezing cold; but on our descending abruptly, the heat increased with every step, as did our hunger in almost equal proportion. At the foot of one of these hills I procured, at an extravagant price, a loaf, and some onions, whereof I ate most heartily.

But my privations (although such as would be reckoned severe by those who have never experienced a state of warfare) were literally nothing compared with the miseries of the unfortunate wounded. Of these, the condition was truly pitiable. Many, after struggling with their fate for some days, gave in at last, and from want of food and exhaustion relinquished all hope of keeping up with the army, and awaited death on the high road; whilst others, famished and dejected, still endeavoured to limp on after their wagons had been broken down,

At the distance of two leagues further we reached our new bivouac under the shelter of oak trees, and here we remained lying throughout the next day, during which we received for the first time since leaving Talavera rations of bread and meat; the former of which was in the shape of sea-biscuit; this supply, however well-timed and salutary, was nevertheless no more than a quarter-allowance.

On the 9th of August, we resumed our progress, and arrived at a village called Jecazego, which (as is common with Spanish hamlets) consisted of a church and a few wretched little huts. The church was now, however, turned into a stable, and in the village not even a drink of water was to be found. We halted at this place a couple of days, and were accommodated by the distribution of provisions, added to which suttlers provided us, from Truxillo, with chocolate, sugar, &c.

On the 12th, we marched three leagues further, and passed by the above-named town, which is large and situated close to a hill. We now rejoined the main army which was quartered in a firm position at Delleytosa, (particularly selected by Lord Wellington,) and where it remained till the 18th. The bridge of Almarez was in our front. Our rearguard, which had been left on the other side of the Tagus, now joined us; having, in the passage of the bridge of Arzobispo, been so hard pushed by the enemy as to occasion the loss of several regiments. The troops of Cuesta had subsequently held possession of the bridge.

We were certainly at length secure both from the attacks of the enemy and from the pressure of absolute want; but now a fresh calamity threatened us, namely, the danger of fire! The ferocious heat had so completely dried up all the grass, roots, &c. that the ground was frequently ignited by our cooking-fires, and in a short time a circumference of several leagues (particularly where the influence of the wind was felt) exhibited one flaming mass.

On the first day of this truly infernal bivouac I myself nearly fell a victim to the fire occasioned by my cookery. I hastened to loosen my horse, which was fastened to a tree hard by; but before I could succeed in unbinding him, the surrounding trusses of hay had kindled, and the greedy flames were mounting high beside me. Against this kind of warfare there was no contending. In some instances, it not only annoyed but deceived us. A day or two after our arrival there arose a universal cry that the enemy was at hand, and had already crossed the bridge of Almarez! whereas, upon further scrutiny, it turned out to be a false alarm, proceeding from an extensive fire in the encampment of the artillery, who were consequently necessitated to change their ground.

Nor was the plague of fire our only evil. The state of clothing amongst the troops had. become deplorable, and was most painfully felt as regarded shoes. The wives of the English soldiers, who were in general so neat and cleanly, were now completely barefooted and with scarce a whole garment, and seated on meagre crazy-footed donkeys, cut a figure altogether forlorn. Many store-wagons had been left behind in the mountains, either owing to their having broken down or to the slaughter of the oxen which drew them, whom the impatient soldiers had greedily butchered; thus allaying the cravings of their stomachs at the expense of their backs and feet From the same cause, numbers of sick and wounded were deprived of their conveyances and forced upon the melancholy alternative of sinking upon the inhospitable soil, or urging their lacerated limbs to excruciating labour.

Thus have we traced the footsteps of carnage, famine, and fire; we have now to record the devastations of pestilence. Diarrhoea, engendered by the spare and unwholesome diet in conjunction with the overpowering heat, tormented our squalid host; and the horses suffered acutely from their long journeys upon a hard, dry, and burning ground.

The biscuit had grown so indurated that it was scarcely possible to moisten it; and (although it was unwise, amidst so many real evils, to conjure up imaginary ones) we could not avoid regretting the want of knives, forks, and spoons, in the absence whereof, the scanty supplies afforded us could not be carried decently to our lips! Our water was furnished by stagnant ditches full of leeches, &c. which got into the nostrils of the horses and into the throats of the men, occasioning perpetual bleeding. Whenever we were fortunate enough to meet with a running stream, we at once used it for purposes of washing, bathing, and drinking.

Nor was there any alleviation from refreshing showers. The baked earth reflected the sultriness which had been communicated to it, and the longer the heats continued the more unbearable did they thence become. If now and then symptoms of tempest appeared in the western heavens, the welcome masses were attracted towards the distant mountains, where they spent their force without favouring our neighbourhood with a single rain-drop, and the air, instead of freshening, waxed yet closer.

The water we drank, being milk-warm, allayed not the thirst, but on the contrary relaxed and weakened our bodies, which wore the pallid aspect of fever-stricken men; and in addition to all, we were well-nigh maddened (day and night) by swarms of noxious insects—such as ants, efts, spiders, locusts, &c. among the latter of which some measured half a yard in length, and were not backward in defending themselves, when resisted, by springing at the person's head.

On the 17th of August, these evils had reached an alarming height. On the 18th, thank God! we broke up at four o'clock in the morning. We did not start, however, until seven—bread, rice, and flour having been previously distributed, although sparingly, to the men. We turned towards the Portuguese frontiers, and in so doing, our leader met the wishes of every one (I believe) amongst his troops, who were completely tired of this inactive and distressing life. Want of provisions was the ostensible cause for the abandonment of this position.

Our route lay in the first place some leagues across the mountains, and at nightfall we halted in a valley near a small river. During the whole day's march, we had perceived no sign of habitation. Our cavalry (formerly such a fine body) presented now a most mournful aspect: instead of eighty, each company was reduced to the possession of about thirty horses, and these regular scarecrows. A great many were led along behind the regiments, and every morning it was found necessary to shoot several of them.

Beside the little stream above-mentioned, we lay encamped two days, during which our situation altered greatly for the better. The heat relaxed on the setting in of a brisk easterly wind—the water was fresher; and we at length breathed freely once more. The bread, which had been for some time limited to quarter-rations, was now advanced to double the quantity—of meat we had a sufficiency, and coffee was brought for sale from a neighbouring place.

On the 20th of August, decisive orders were issued to march upon Portugal. The dragoons and hussars dismounted and fastened their accoutrements between the horns of the oxen, troops of which were attached to each brigade, nor did the animals seem at all displeased with this novel decoration. I had formerly stigmatized as insufferable the dilatoriness of the Spaniards and Portuguese: but in this quality they were now rivalled by ourselves; for none of us felt inclined to move, except from the pressure of necessity. Our horses, at the commencement of the campaign full of fire and energy, now dropped their ears and looked listless and dispirited.

We had become heedless as to the particular marking of time. A man scarcely cared to wind up his watch; and instead of specifying the hour, it was common to say "We shall march at daybreak." With regard to the day of the week, all calculation of that matter had long been abandoned.

Having continued our route five leagues across a mountainous country, we proceeded three leagues further through a desert heath, as far as Caceres, where we bivouacked on a hill upon stony ground.

Caceres is an ancient town, lying upon a height, but not very large. The houses are massive, and generally speaking sadly out of repair: the streets narrow, and the shops looking like so many cellars. The market-place presents a ruinous archway, but it is plentifully stocked. There were abundance of coffee-houses and pastry-cooks' shops, but what I wanted was a substantial meal, and this I could not succeed in procuring.

On the 23rd we marched onwards, and halted near another small town; and on this day we again received, after a considerable interval, our full rations of bread, meat, and wine. Hardly, however, had we gained time to provide our meal, when orders came to proceed further, at five o'clock p. m. By eight the moon became overcast, and we had to blunder on in the dark: and our water being exhausted, we were ultimately obliged to lie down amongst the bushes with parched tongues.

Pursuing our retreat in this way, we reached, on the 27th of August, the important border-fortress of Badajos, and encamped on the banks of the Guadiana, and there we halted during the following day. From hence the eye easily commands the neighbouring stronghold of Elvas, which is situate upon a high hill, and displays an aspect both picturesque and imposing. Badajos itself stands upon rising ground in the middle of a wide plain, and is regularly built.

The streets are broad, but in bad condition. There was an air of spirit and order about this place; and the houses were well furnished and even cleanly. Provisions, also, were to be had of every description; and, on the whole, Badajos did a great deal towards reconciling us to Spain.

Fording the Guadiana, which here forms the boundary-line

between the sister-kingdoms, we passed by Elvas, and proceeded until we arrived at the Royal Menagerie, (not far from Villaviciosa,) which is several leagues in circumference, and surrounded by a wall eighteen feet high.

Through this enclosure, in order to save a circuitous route, we were permitted to pass; and half a league on the other side of it we came to the fine town of Villaviciosa, which contains a very handsome palace. Hence we proceeded a mile or two further to the agreeable town of Borba, where our regiment bivouacked in the garden of a monastery.

Chapter 19

Autumn in Spain

At length we seemed to have arrived at a resting-point, after our calamitous retreat, and once more found ourselves in pleasant quarters. It is true, our sleeping accommodations were none of the best, although the fragrant trees of the gardens overcanopied us, for the ground was arid, and strewed some inches thick with dust. The meanest hut would have been a luxury,—but was not to be procured.

After awhile circumstances permitted me to remove into the town of Borba, where I took lodgings. Those who have never had similar experience would find it difficult to imagine the delight felt by me on once more entering a comfortable bed. With what alacrity did I take my seat, in. the morning, at a breakfast-table furnished with wholesome bread and butter, &c. in lieu of the eternal chocolate, brewed in a dusty can, which used to grate upon my teeth as I drank it!

The difference was exceedingly perceptible between the Portuguese and Spanish border-places, as regarded almost every matter of convenience: added to which; the civility of the inhabitants of Portugal formed a most agreeable contrast to the cold hauteur of the Spaniards. From Badajos hither, the look of the towns and villages was livelier, the houses being generally white-washed; whilst in Spain they wore an appearance of decided gloom. Borba, where we hoped to stay long enough to effect our restoration, really afforded very desirable quarters.

The town lies in a fruitful plain of Alentejo, is middle-sized, and built with much regularity. The churches, monasteries, &c. are numerous; and the whole wears a look of importance, which may perhaps be accounted for, by its having been, formerly, the summer residence of the Portuguese kings.

On the heels of this improvement in our situation, came a refreshing rain, which, after the preceding drought of two months, was extremely acceptable. Throughout the whole of this short campaign, and particularly during our retreat, all manner of diseases had grown familiar to our troops—cold, fever, jaundice, diarrhoea, &c. I had, however, escaped miraculously from either; but now, the sudden transition from incessant fatigue to a state of repose, brought on unpleasant symptoms, and especially pains in the legs, which attacked me severely in the mornings.

A supposition had been started that our regiment, owing to its serious losses, would be sent back to England: but this soon proved incorrect, the 23rd Dragoons being the only regiment so disposed of, which was replaced by the 16th Dragoons, who formed a brigade in conjunction with us. Shortly after this arrangement, orders were received to prepare again for active service; though how it was to be done did not plainly appear, since our regiment had lost a hundred men and double that; number of horses, and even the remainder were sick and wretched.

Nor were the other cavalry regiments in better plight, whilst nearly the whole of the infantry were lying in the hospitals, having suffered much more than the cavalry. The garments of the men were in a tattered condition, the military stores, &c. very deficient, and time would, at any rate, be requisite to replace the equipments of the army from England. The spirits of our troops were also damped on account of the disastrous result of their exertions at Talavera; and nothing seemed to afford them satisfaction but the notion of Lord Wellington's remaining some time on the frontier, to defend the kingdom of Portugal. Indeed, this was little to be wondered at, when we consider the quarters occupied here by a portion of the army.

One of the hospitals, for instance, was established in the hotel of a nobleman, wherein every luxury was accumulated which was desirable in a southern climate. At the back of the house stretched a delicious garden, containing a profusion of the finest fruits and flowers. Cool marble grottoes and fountains yielding the most pellucid water, (which streamed through the place[1]) lent their aid to the other enchantments of this spot, the whole of which was enclosed by a box-hedge, five feet in height, and tortured into a variety of figures, according to the taste now happily exploded. I never, in the course of my life, beheld such magnificent lemons as were to be met with in this earthly paradise, some of them equalling in size the head of a child a couple of years old.

In consequence of the rain, it grew a little cooler; whereupon the Portuguese gentlemen immediately produced their huge wrapping-cloaks, and the ladies their mantles, to which is commonly added a long veil, reaching very low down the back and utterly concealing the face, whence their costume has something about it of an Eastern character.

On the 5th of September, 1809, after these few days' halt, the regiment was already in motion, retracing its steps into the adjoining kingdom. Our sick, to the number of eighty, were conveyed from Borba to Villaviciosa, where they were deposited in a hospital which had once been a royal palace:—I call it a hospital, as the rooms were emptied for that purpose; but there was neither chair, table, nor bed. The removal of these poor fellows occasioned them much torture, in consequence of the miserable conveyance, whereby they were kept upon the road a whole day!

In Elvas, the case was very different. The British hospital there was in an extensive Franciscan monastery, the greatest part whereof had been evacuated by the monks for the use of the sick and wounded. Far more room was, it is true, wanted to receive the numbers every day brought in; but those who did find accommodation there, derived from the truly Christian benevolence of the lay-brothers and superior monks, all the alleviation

1. This is peculiar to the gardens of Portugal, which are thus irrigated by means of marble ducts.

of which their state was susceptible. In the garden appertaining to this holy convent was a representation of the crucifixion curiously cut out in box!

On the 9th of September I proceeded to Badajos, the weather having again become intolerably hot. As it chanced to be Sunday, I strolled into the principal church of that town, where mass was celebrating with no small splendour. The walls and pillars were hung with velvet, and the floor was of marble. I was much struck with the pensive-looking sweetness of the female devotees, whose slim figures occasionally peeped forth from the ample veils which, as I have already described, reach below their waists.

At La Roca, a gloomy-looking collection of some couple of hundred huts dignified with the name of a town, and situated in a barren country where nothing could be got but prisoner's fare—bread and water, we halted from the 10th of September to the 1st of October, for the purpose of further recruiting our strength against the ensuing campaign. Here the efforts of the tailors and shoemakers of the place, assisted by those of our own artisans, were put in active requisition to repair our respective wardrobes, since fresh clothes were not to be thought of; and by the time this was effected we had grown heartily sick both of our quarters and of our inactivity.

My readers will duly estimate the fascinations of this lively place when I inform them the houses were, in height, from twelve to sixteen feet; containing no glazed windows, in place whereof were holes fastened on occasion by shatters—so that, if a man wanted either air or light, he was necessitated to give entrance at the same time to a host of pestiferous insects. The inhabitants are in excellent keeping with the character of the place—looking as yellow as their lemons and as withered as their soil.

On the 1st of October a party of our regiment, including myself, proceeded to Valverde, in Spanish Estremadura, where we fell in with another battalion of it, and had a very pleasant sojourn until the 20th instant. This proved quite another guess place from La Roca, being built upon high ground, containing good houses and opulent inhabitants, and having hitherto been unmolested by the presence of any army either of friends or foes. Individually, however, I had no great cause to be pleased with my reception here, as I was the occasion of ejecting a priest from his dwelling who had occupied it already half a century.

My residence in Valverde gave me opportunity of ascertaining more fully the character of the higher orders of the Spanish people, many of whom lived therein, and whom I found almost uniformly over-rating their own importance. It was easy to distinguish the abodes of the *nobiles* and *dons* by the escutcheon which, skilfully carved and gaudily painted, surmounted the entrance of their palaces.

I had the honour of being invited to sundry balls during my stay, whereat I found the ladies elegantly dressed, whilst the men still retained the short jacket, over which was thrown the eternal cloak! Thus accoutred, with the addition of an old three-cornered hat and a lighted cigar (wherewith his mouth is rarely unaccommodated) the Spanish cavalier cuts a most dirty and negligent figure. Their *contre-danse* displayed considerable grace and abundant gesticulation; but the *fandango* was the established favourite.

Still a number of my comrades continued to lie in La Roca, whither I made frequent visits, and from whence the troops did not break up till the end of the year; and meanwhile I availed myself of the opportunities afforded of observing upon the customs and manners of the people. I frequently met in my excursions parties of upwards of twenty mules, &c. whereupon whole families travelled from one place to another, the ladies seated upon pillions highly decorated and softly padded, and having leaning places for both ride and back. This train proceeded generally in a slow measured pace, consistent with the gravity of the Spanish character.

The little caravan was escorted by a guide, and the men belonging to it were all provided with arms. Sumpter-mules were also in attendance, laden, among other things, with cooking utensils—an arrangement originating partly in the ostentation of the travellers and partly in the real necessity springing from the paucity and bad accommodations of the inns, particularly in that province.

Thus, on arriving towards night at any place where none of their connexions are established, instead of seeking a house of entertainment, they pitch their tents in the open air, and without repining begin preparations for their evening meal. Not that there is any lack in Spain of the spirit of hospitality; on the contrary, it is often extended to the meanest stranger; but as frequently does the uncongenial feeling of pride interfere to prevent its acceptance.

The method of burying the dead in Spain and Portugal may seem strange to many: no coffins are used, nor indeed the customary shroud; the body is carried into the church in an open box or chest; the church is lighted up, and the officiating priest pronounces a *benedicie* over the departed. In this manner a couple of our hussars were dealt with, whom, in order to secure them any funeral rites at all, we were compelled to pass off as having been good Catholics.

In the beginning of November the summer heats had relaxed, and rendered the weather, although still rather too warm at midday, agreeable enough, particularly in the mornings and evenings. The salutary dews, accompanied by a fall of rain, made the face of Nature green and verdant, and the labourers were hard at work in the fields. But before the month had concluded, the Spanish winter set in with some degree of severity. The natives crept close to their fires; whilst thick masses of cloud obscured the heretofore brilliant azure, and damp, chill blasts contributed to depress the mental as well as bodily energies.

This latter inconvenience was however soon removed by one or two thunder-storms, which were succeeded by clear cheerful weather: the fig-trees and vines had, by this time, been deflowered of their leaves, but the oaks, lemon, and orange trees still bloomed in undecaying beauty. In December the nights had become exceedingly bitter: ice was frequently generated an inch thick, but it disappeared on the sun gaining his meridian, when his influence was still sufficient to tempt the women out of their huts, in order to bask in the welcome warmth whilst they plied their spindles.

At length instructions were issued, by virtue whereof we were to march from La Roca for the northern part of Portugal, which was threatened by the enemy. Our stay at the former place had proved effectual as to supplying us with the repairs, &c. necessary for a fresh campaign: and (owing more to the coolness of the air than any other cause) our horses had likewise benefited greatly. The stated numbers of the regiment, however, had not, according to anticipation, been filled up.

Lord Wellington's plan had been, it seems, since the battle of Talavera, to proceed in his measures without the co-operation of the Spanish army, until it should be better organised. He, however, would not withdraw his forces from Spain until circumstances (as was now the case) rendered such a step incumbent on him, and even then his intention was to take such a position on the frontiers as might enable him at once to defend Portugal and continue close to Spain. The army had, therefore, in compliance with this view of things, lain so long between Merida and Badajos; but its presence had now become requisite elsewhere.

Chapter 20

Visit of Lord Wellington

We marched over a considerable tract of country, passing in succession several of the best towns in Portugal, such as Portalegre, which, like Rome, might be called "the city built on seven hills,"—Coimbra, celebrated for containing the only university in the kingdom,—and Abrantes, at which place nearly the whole of the English army formed a junction: and finally arrived at Guarda on the 11th of January, where a large portion of the army (among which was a battalion of our regiment) took up its winter quarters. The remainder of the English forces were distributed in other places in the province of Beira, and the chief quarters were established at Viseu. The division of General Hill continued, however, to lie upon the bank of the Tagus.

On the 13th of January, Lord Wellington paid a visit to Guarda, in order to muster the troops, and learn their exact situation. His arrival was the signal for the liveliest demonstrations of joy, which were expressed in illuminations, ringing of bells, &c. During the period of our stay in this place, the army was recruited in every possible way; in numbers, in spirits, in wealth, and in clothing; and it remained here until the middle of March.

Towards the end of February, the enemy showed himself before the frontier town of Ciudad Rodrigo, and in consequence out-posts were established to watch his movements. Meanwhile, Portuguese recruits marched constantly through Guarda, to join their different corps, and not yet being duly equipped, were covered in many instances with mantles actually of straw, which, although destitute of any shapeliness whatever, yet served well enough as a shield against the inclemency of the weather. One could easily distinguish in these men, speaking generally, their African descent; as they had thick lips, indented foreheads, turn-up noses, and jet-black hair.

The Portuguese army having, in consequence of the indefatigable exertions of Marshal Beresford, been got into perfect discipline, established its junction with the British forces, and occupied an extended line reaching from the Tagus to the Douro. The appointment of English officers to the Portuguese troops contributed more than any other circumstance to reduce them from a state of great disorder to equally conspicuous regularity.

On the 17th of March, 1810, the army was once more in motion. Late at night, after a march of five leagues across a mountainous country, we reached the small town of Castelmande close to the frontiers. The fortress of Almeida is situated in the immediate vicinity.

On the 19th inst. the French commenced offensive operations by an attack upon the only bridge, near St. Felices, (two leagues from Gallegos,) across the Agunda. It was occupied by four companies of the English Ninety-Fifth Regiment of Light Infantry, whose piquets were established on the opposite shore. These outposts were driven back over the bridge with the loss of an officer and thirteen privates.

The remainder of the regiment, which had been lying at the village of Barba del Puerco, having come up on the following day, the enemy's party, in number about 600, were in turn repulsed. The hostile forces, indeed, were generally speaking impeded in their advance upon Ciudad Rodrigo by the inundated state of the roads in consequence of the heavy rains which fell about this time. On the 30th, our Spanish allies who had sent out a reconnoitring party made thirty prisoners, the heterogeneous nature of which small company was curious enough, as it included Frenchmen, Italians, Germans, and Dutch.

After a variety of demonstrations on the part of the enemy, who showed himself here and there and was closely watched in his movements by the commanders of the allied army, (whence our removal from one spot to another was rendered frequently necessary,) he, on the 25th of May, without having fired a shot against the fortress of Ciudad Rodrigo, required its unconditional surrender, and it was plainly to be seen that Lord Wellington felt no disposition to risk anything in the defence of that place, as the infantry was suffered to remain a league in its rear, and only the cavalry and mounted artillery retained the neighbouring position of Gallegos.

About this period, our regiment received an addition of some 200 men, together with fresh horses, from England. My own station during these events was at Castelbon, a place upon the border, and perched as it were upon the very loftiest point of these heights. Here I remained in uninterrupted tranquillity until the middle of June.

The peculiar situation of Castelbon merits notice. It might, doubtless, have formerly served as a place of imprisonment for political offenders or persons suspected by the government. It is approached only by one road, extremely narrow, and overhung by precipices which seem every moment to threaten the passenger like the sword which hung over the head of the friend of Dionysius, and upon the points whereof the wild goats are to be seen gazing with a look of stupid astonishment upon the travellers underneath.

The ancient castle is in utter ruins; whilst the savage aspect of the surrounding country is in thorough keeping with its look of desolation. During the rainy season, the rocks are visited by brawling cataracts, which, forming for themselves rude channels, rush with headlong precipitation into the adjoining Coa, which, river, with similar impetuosity, forces itself upwards through a confined and stony bed. This stream, when viewed from the heights, appears within gunshot distance, but a stranger would be surprised on finding the route so circuitous as to cause an hour's expenditure in reaching it.

The underwood springing up through the fissures of the rocks is, curiously enough, resorted to by flocks of nightingales, whose somewhat pensive melody heightens the romantic character of this wild region, where even in the month of June, after the air has been cleared by a thunder-storm, the cold is felt quite severely.

On the 9th of June, the enemy threw a bridge of boats over the Aquada, drove back our piquets, and to all appearance was disposed seriously to lay siege to Ciudad Rodrigo. Still, however, he seemed not to like the vicinity of our army; and the rainy weather contributed, by deluging the roads, to check his movements. He was straitened also from want of provisions, the due supply of which was cut off by parties of the Spaniards. At length, the atmosphere grew cloudless, and thus, one principal obstacle being removed, upon the 15th of June, on which day Marshal Massena assumed the chief command of the French army, their trenches were opened against the Spanish fortress.

Before Massena had quitted Salamanca, for the purpose abovementioned, he issued a proclamation wherein he was pleased to style himself King of Portugal, and according to his usual pompous way promised that he would, within three months, drive the English army into the sea! At the same time, he commanded (by virtue of his assumed sovereignty) that every English officer who should be captured bearing commission in the Portuguese service, should be forthwith hanged; whereupon Lord Wellington perceived the necessity of threatening, by way of retaliation, the execution of two French officers for every British one.

On the 18th of June I visited Fuentes D'Onore, where was established a branch of the commissariat department. The flour provided for the troops had been imported from America, and the Turkish corn, as well as the cattle, from Africa!—from which circumstances the reader may form some judgement of the expense entailed by this war upon the British nation. Here, we could distinguish plainly enough the noise arising from the bombardment of Ciudad Rodrigo, which was distant about two leagues. Meanwhile our outposts were constantly skirmishing with the enemy, and parties of wounded were daily brought in.

Lord Wellington had apparently renounced all intention of

relieving the besieged fortress. In fact, the British army was too weak to contend against the hostile force, which on its advance towards Portugal was estimated at 110,000 men, whilst the allies did not exceed, in number, 60,000, whereof, also, the greater part consisted of inexperienced Portuguese. In the Spanish corps which, under General Carara, passed about this time through Fuentes, were several Spanish women of rank, who to our no small amusement were habited in breeches, and rode astride, like the men.

It is worthy of remark that, in a border-country, where it should seem that national differences between the adjoining races would be least apparent, it is (at any rate in the instance before us) most so. The Spanish peasants are a good deal handsomer than the Portuguese, and both the one and the other wear garments of the coarsest woollen stuff, in spite of the beautiful fleeces yielded by their sheep. This deficiency is accounted for by the imperfection of their method of manufacture—the spindle universally made use of not furnishing those fine threads produced by more elaborate machinery.

On the 25th of June, the besiegers opened a fire from forty-six pieces of artillery of the greatest calibre; and although at a distance of two leagues, the effects of this fire and of a subsequent explosion were so manifest as to awaken me from a very comfortable sleep by bringing down the plaster from the roof of my apartment,

On the 27th of June, I was obliged to leave Fuentes, as a part of our regiment which had been engaged during the whole of the spring upon piquet duty was removed, in order to recover their fatigue, into the rear. Accordingly, we marched successively to Castelbon, to Frexeda across the Coa bridge, and (on the 29th) to Marca de Cahoe, (near Celerico,) the inhabitants of which wretched-looking place were running about almost naked. Here and in Minhocal we remained until the 5th of July.

It may not be amiss at this point of my narrative to describe the existing circumstances of the allied army.—The head-quarters of the commander-in-chief were established at Alverca, a large village, one league from Minhocal. The forces were divided into five corps, which were distributed as follows:—one under General Hill lay on the banks of the Tagus; a second, commanded by General Spencer, was stationed near Celerico; a third, under General Cole, occupied Guarda and its neighbourhood; a fourth, at the head of which was General Picton, lay in the vicinity of Pinhel; whilst the remaining division, as an advanced corps, occupied Gallegos, and was commanded by General Crawford: to this latter, was attached the battalion wherein I served. On the 4th of July, General Crawford's division was forced back by the enemy, to prevent its interference with his designs upon Ciudad Rodrigo; and on this occasion, a brother-officer of mine particularly distinguished himself, having with his single company held at bay thirty French squadrons of cavalry, near a bridge over a small river, thereby preventing the loss of a body of artillery.

Meantime, the fortress of Ciudad Rodrigo; after an heroic resistance on the part of its governor, General Herrasti, and the garrison and inhabitants, fell by assault; and its fall rendered our situation more critical. Up to the 24th instant, General Crawfurd had maintained his position; but on that day the enemy advanced, and forced him, with considerable loss, beyond Almeida to Carvalhal. In our retreat we demolished the fort La Conception, and immediately after, the hostile troops invested Almeida.

Chapter 21

Treachery of Massena

Having sufficiently refreshed itself in the interim, our battalion resumed its activity on the 25th instant, by advancing to the village of Balge, and upon its road thither was joined by a division of the 16th English Light Dragoons. At Balge we continued up to the 21st of August; but during this interval we could not reckon on remaining undisturbed from one day to another, but passed the nights with our knapsacks under our heads, and our caps and swords by our side. The inhabitants of the place had been ordered to repair to the mountains—an intimation altogether unnecessary, since their flight had, in fact, preceded it.

In the meanwhile the defence of Almeida appeared to rival in its obstinacy that of Ciudad Rodrigo. Lord Wellington was not, however, on this occasion equally inactive, for on the 21st instant we found the main army had advanced and was close behind us. From Balge we proceeded to the village of Bardiebe, before which we encamped.

Thus posted, the army was stationary until the 27th, expecting every moment orders for proceeding to attack the enemy. As it turned out, however, this was nothing more than a feint of the English general, in order to frustrate a plan of Marshal Massena, in pursuance whereof he had detached a corps under Junot either to penetrate into Portugal and intercept Lord Wellington's retreat, or at least to induce him to fall back upon Lisbon. By his Lordship's advance this hopeful scheme was altogether outmanoeuvred, since the French marshal, without loss of time, recalled the corps of Junot.

Almeida fell, chiefly, as was currently stated, owing to the pusillanimity of the Portuguese governor, Da Costa, and the chief of artillery, Barreros, against whose united weakness the bravery of the English commandant of the garrison, Colonel Cox, vainly strove. In fact, the colonel had reason to congratulate himself, under the pressure of these adverse circumstances, upon obtaining a favourable capitulation, which, however, was not fulfilled by Massena, who retained in his hands six hundred of the Portuguese militia, contrary to stipulation.

A series of movements followed this event, accompanied by occasional skirmishing, and undertaken by the English general for the purpose of facilitating his retreat, which was conducted in good order until we found ourselves upon the Sierra de Busaco, in a position taken up in order to cover Coimbra. Our regiment lay towards the base of this chain of mountains, and after having remained there awhile we received orders to fall back half a league, where we passed the night under olive-trees. Next morning, however, we resumed our position.

On the 25th of September the enemy made several attacks, early in the morning, upon our fight troops, but without any success, being driven back by Generals Crawfurd and Pack, without considerable loss. But it was not till two days after that Massena directed his great efforts towards the defeat of the undervalued English army. These efforts were principally expended upon the wings of the allied force, and were conducted by Generals Simon and Graindorge, at the head of the 2nd and 6th corps of the enemy. The assault upon the right wing, which was commanded by Major-General Picton, took place at six o'clock in the morning.

One of the French divisions attained the summit of the hill, which was occupied by the 45th and 88th English and the 8th Portuguese regiments, which succeeded in repulsing their assailants at the point of the bayonet. Another hostile division did not attain the height, but was driven back by the 74th English regiment and a brigade of Portuguese. The corps whereby the left of our army was attacked had been separated into three divisions, against which Generals Crawfurd and Pack were opposed, who likewise overcame their antagonists, hurling them back, as they successively advanced, at the head of the 48th, 54th, and 95th English and 3rd Portuguese regiments.

Towards afternoon a truce was established for a couple of hours, in order to remove the wounded on both sides; during which my duty led me to ascend the utmost ridge of the Sierra, upon which a convent is situated, wherein the hapless Queen Matilda of Portugal once took up her residence. This picturesque spot, which commanded a thorough view of the scene of operations, was now the head-quarters of Lord Wellington; and from it the prospect was most interesting—upwards of 150,000 warriors, of various nations, lying upon the sides of the mountains, just reeking with the fatigue of attack or defence, and ready to engage again at the appointed signal.

So close was the enemy's position to our own, that with the help of an ordinary telescope individuals might with ease be distinguished upon the opposite heights. The French outposts were established so near to the foot of our hill that they were within a stone's throw: one of them, indeed, was held by General Crawfurd to be imprudently contiguous; and that humane general sent by an *aide-de-camp* to the officer commanding it an intimation to that effect: but as it was disregarded, no sooner had the truce expired, than this piquet was swept away by a discharge of artillery.

These offensive operations of the French marshal cost him very dear; and the general opinion was, that nothing short of insanity could excuse his rashness. He now abandoned all thoughts of penetrating at this point; but it was soon observed, that he sent strong parties to occupy the road leading from Oporto to Coimbra, hoping, by that means, to outflank Lord Wellington.

In consequence of this demonstration, an officer of our regiment was despatched with a battalion, late in the afternoon, up mountainous by-roads, to Colonel Trant, who was commanding in the environs of Oporto, directing him to march, without loss of time, to the pass of Sardao; and by maintaining that post, prevent the enemy's gaining his object. Colonel Trant, however, was too late in his expedition, as, on account of an hostile corps, which held possession of San Pedro de Sal, he was forced to take a circuitous route.

On the evening of the 28th, the whole French army broke up, and took the direction of the road to our left. Our regiment was instructed to advance against him by the way of Annadeo, and after a very disagreeable march, partly in total darkness, we bivouacked, at ten o'clock, near a small village.

On the following day, our patrols fell in with the enemy, and according to orders, we immediately fell back two leagues, as far as Mortagao, a place lying on the road to Oporto, and through which we had passed, in the spring, on our march to Guarda. Here we were joined by the 16th English Dragoons. On the 30th of September, by dawn of day, we were attacked by the enemy under circumstances which appeared to me peculiarly disagreeable, as I was aroused from a comfortable breakfast. Both regiments drew slowly back, keeping up, as they retreated, a running fire. By midday we had retired several leagues on the road to Coimbra; and, as the enemy had apparently given over his pursuit, we halted beneath the shade of a grove of olives.

This luxuriant country bad been unexpectedly overrun by the hostile forces; and whilst yet the luscious fruits fairly weighed down the boughs on which they hung, the unfortunate inhabitants felt themselves compelled to abandon their homes, strapping a few valuables upon their backs, and leading, by the hand, their terrified children, whose down cast, yet inquiring looks, appeared to seek an explanation of circumstances which, happily for them, they could neither fully understand nor appreciate.

The 1st of October, 1810, was an inauspicious day for Portugal, whose defenders then perceived the necessity of abandoning Coimbra and the Mondego, and falling back upon the distant lines near Lisbon. Early in the morning I was led by business to the former town, which I found wrapt in a state of the utmost consternation. "The enemy is at the gate!" was the perpetual cry:

and that part of the inhabitants which remained were seduced, by their fears, into the belief of all manner of improbable things. During my stay here, a number of wounded, belonging to our regiment, were brought in, and conducted to the market-place, amidst the shrieks and lamentations of the townsfolk.

The condition of this city formed indeed, altogether, a mournful and striking illustration of the miseries of war! A number of houses were left quite open and unprotected, the rooms containing abundance of valuable furniture: excepting in that part of the town where the military were collected, (around whom the citizens all flocked,) the silence of death reigned in the streets;—and so great was the universal dread of the French, that invalids were brought to us by their friends, who solicited us to take them under our protection, as they were fearful of absolute massacre.

Towards ten o'clock, we also quitted this devoted city, marching across the bridge over the Mondego, whereof the middle arch was immediately after demolished. For awhile we pursued our course quietly, and in good order; but the road soon became so thronged with fugitives, wearied soldiers, (belonging to the divisions of infantry which had preceded us,) baggage-wagons, laden mules, &c. that it became absolutely blocked up.

Next morning early, our corps, consisting of 6000 men, proceeded five leagues further back in the direction of Pombal. Dust and heat increased daily in the southern part of the country, but the nights were cool—nay, even cold. In the course of the day, the greater part of the English army assembled at Pombal, and encamped in the neighbourhood of that place. The dark night which followed was grotesquely illumined by the countless multitude of cooking fires which lighted up the country to the extent of several leagues. On the following day, the entire army marched within two leagues of Leiria, and here the light brigade of cavalry, which had crossed the river near Coimbra, rejoined us.

On the 4th inst. I received orders to proceed, with a corps of sick and wounded, to Lisbon, whilst the light cavalry was appointed to keep the enemy at bay, and thereby to favour as much as possible the retreat of the British army to its lines of entrenchment

On arriving at Leiria towards midday, I found that otherwise pleasant town a prey to all the horrors of war. Instructions had been issued to the inhabitants to make their escape, which sundry false and exaggerated rumours caused them to accomplish with inconvenient and unnecessary speed. The authors of these reports were, in most instances, scoundrels who took advantage of the unhappy state of circumstances to rifle the houses of the terrified citizens.

During the disorder attendant on these scenes of suffering and atrocity, Lord Wellington arrived; and his presence tended at once to assuage the tumult. The brigands were several of them arrested; and two of the principal culprits, one of whom was in the English and the other in the Portuguese service, hung upon trees outside the town, where their bodies were kept until the whole of the army had passed, as a warning to the rest of the soldiers.

The confusion prevailing in the streets of Leiria was extraordinary, and presented a spectacle of mournful interest. Sugar, coffee, and chocolate, and other articles of merchandise, were strewed lavishly about upon the ground, whilst many of the inhabitants of the place were still occupied in collecting their most valuable property, to rescue it, if possible, from the enemy's hands.

On entering one of the houses, I found a man whom from his rigid posture and vacant stare, I scarcely imagined to be alive. He made no answer to my salutations, nor could I get him to rise from the chair whereon he sate. I passed on to see if there were any other inmates of this gloomy abode, and discovered in an inner apartment a sick person, who was reduced to the last state of exhaustion and debility from the combined effects of illness and want of food, and who told me that he had not received so much as a draught of water during the last two days!

I busied myself to procure some refreshment for this neglected wretch, and having in a measure succeeded, made inquiries concerning the man who evinced such palpable estrangement of mind. My surprise ceased when I learnt that be had been reduced, by the extortions and depredations incidental to the lamentable condition of the country, from comparative affluence to utter destitution!

This retreat of the Anglo-Portuguese army from Coimbra to the entrenchments was, in truth, attended with most disastrous circumstances to the unfortunate people of the region through which it was carried on. Every division of our forces was accompanied by a troop at least equally numerous of fugitives; and it was quite disgusting to observe the alacrity with which our allies pillaged their own fellow-countrymen.

This heterogeneous mass, which appeared to be stimulated by a common feeling of inexpressible horror at the French, comprised rich and poor—men and women—old and young—mothers with their infants either led by the hand or pendent from their backs. Even nuns abandoned their convents; and, strangers in the world around them, vainly sought each some protecting friend or relative. As this melancholy train approached the capital, the horses and mules had most of them become exhausted, and unable to proceed further; and it was no uncommon sight to perceive a richly-clad lady, with silken slippers, wading through the mud of the high road.

The celebrated lines of Torres Vedras, constructed to cover Lisbon, will ever rank amongst the most ingenious and skilful works of the kind. On one side they rested upon the Tagus, which was occupied by English gun-boats, &c.; and on the other, stretched towards the sea. Art had been fairly exhausted in increasing the natural strength of this position: the neighbouring heights had been rendered inaccessible by means of sundry excavations: the adjacent roads were cut through; redoubts, sheltered by ditches and palisades, were constructed—and dams formed whereby the country might, be at will overflowed.

Nearly 400 pieces of artillery were employed in the defence of this entrenchment, which spread over an extent of ten leagues. Thus was Lisbon, by wise precautions, converted into an immense fortress; and upon its continued occupation the fate of the Peninsula appeared to rest.

On the 11th of October, I arrived once more at the suburb of Belem, which, as well as the capital itself, I found much more cleanly and less crowded than I had expected, considering the numbers who flocked hither from the various abandoned towns. The comparative cleanliness was attributable partly to the heavy rains which had recently fallen, and, in a still greater degree, to the salutary regulations of the English police which had been organised here; and to account for the unexpected thinness, it was only necessary to revert to the numbers of able-bodied men which had been marched off to strengthen the lines,—several battalions of whom had passed me on the road.

The houses, it is true, were completely filled: but, judging from the hosts of fugitives whom I had myself encountered on their way to the metropolis, I should have felt no surprise at seeing the streets likewise thoroughly beset! But, although great misery and privation of every kind attended the removal of these unfortunates, yet the fate of those who chose to remain was far more dreadful.

Under pretence of forcing confessions of hidden treasure, the invaders perpetrated the utmost atrocities—the extent and diabolical nature of which are actually unfitted for description. Perhaps the most appalling destiny attended the unoffending inmates of the various nunneries, who, abandoned to the brutal will of the French soldiery, if they escaped with life, generally had to mourn over the irremediable loss of mental tranquillity.

Lisbon, however, afforded a safe, asylum for these bereaved exiles. Temporary houses of wood were erected; and public kitchens provided, where immense quantities of food were cooked and distributed gratis. To meet the expense of these humane arrangements, the British government had appropriated the sum of £100,000; and the English nation, ever forward in acts of generosity, raised, to its immortal honour, a similar sum by subscription.

Various business connected with my professional duties detained me at Belem above five weeks. Here I was excellently lodged, and fared sumptuously every day. The windows of my apartment overlooked the majestic Tagus, upon whose bosom thousands of vessels glanced to and fro, including many large English and Portuguese ships of war and transports. My hotel was served *à l'Anglaise,* with the addition of the choicest wines and fruits indigenous to the country.

This change of circumstances was the more agreeable, and more sensibly felt, when I recollected (as I could not fail to do) the hard quarters I had recently to put up with,—an olive-tree often serving for my canopy, around the trunk whereof innumerable insects and reptiles ensconced themselves as fellow-lodgers,—and my cheerless meal being hastily swallowed upon the ground, plentifully mingled with dust.

As a proof how thoroughly the Portuguese capital was at this time Anglicised, I may add that, on visiting the opera one night, I found the ballet to consist of part of the adventures of Captain Cook, and his death, among the barbarians. The *corps-de-ballet* had little trouble, indeed, in representing the Otaheitan ruffians, for nothing could possibly be more savage than their appearance—except their dancing.

Shortly before the full establishment of the allied forces in the lines at Torres Vedras, a dangerous conspiracy had been fortunately detected by the vigilance of Marshal Beresford. Its object was, in fact, no less than to set fire to the English fleet on the Tagus, and to take advantage of the surprise resulting therefrom, to betray the British army, by attacking it in the rear, whilst Massena should advance in front. Fire-ships, destined for the prosecution of this infernal scheme, were discovered upon the river, whilst a vast depot of arms and equipments was seized in Lisbon.

The confederates in this hopeful plot were, as may be supposed, numerous; upon its detection, they were arrested and sent out of Lisbon; and, during the remainder of my stay, I heard of no other instances of treachery. Meanwhile, in despite of their double hostility, both open and concealed, Lord Wellington firmly maintained his post, and seemed, indeed, as immovable as the hills which contributed to defend it.

That Coimbra would fall into the enemy's hands immediately after its abandonment by the allies was self-evident; but it could not so easily have been foreseen that Colonel Trant should advance upon the town with scarcely any delay, overthrow the French garrison, take possession of the bridge leading across the Mondego, and thus cut off all communication with the enemy's main army.

This latter was, indeed, itself situated in very straitened circumstances. Marshal Massena had, in his advance into Portugal, calculated upon shortly becoming master of Lisbon, particularly as he had established an understanding in that city. He did not contemplate the wasted condition to which the country had been systematically reduced, and therefore was careless of providing large stores.

The impregnable strength of the entrenchments before Lisbon was, likewise, unanticipated by him; and the communication with both France and Spain being cut off by bands of Portuguese guerillas, the French army perceived itself to be in a very disagreeable situation.

The Marshal complained most bitterly of the spoliation of the country, which he termed a specimen of Indian, and not of civilized warfare; and he commanded the inhabitants,[1] on pain of death, to return to their dwellings. The English reconnoitring parties, under the command of General Miller and Colonel Trant, frequently brought in a number of the enemy's foragers. Numerous deserters, likewise, came over to our outposts, averring that they were on the point of starvation; and to these poor fellows was given a portion of Turkish corn, which they broke between two stones, and having baked it in a pan, greedily devoured.

1. These poor people were driven into a dilemma, which would be ludicrous, were not the subject so grave. The Portuguese government, backed by the authority of the British commander-in-chief, directed them to abandon their homes; whilst the French leader enjoined them to continue therein under the most frightful penalties, which compliance (I am sorry to say) was not always effectual in averting.

The festival of All Souls (Nov. 2nd), I attended high mass in the royal chapel, situated upon the highest point of Buenos Ayres, of which eminence the reader will find some description in chapter 14. The ceremony was performed, on this occasion, by the patriarch himself, in character of prime dignitary of the Portuguese clergy.

The chapel is not of large dimensions, but decorated with great splendour. The altars are adorned most magnificently, and the organ-pipes are of silver; the orchestra, which accompanied this grand mass with both vocal and instrumental music, included, among the choir, a profusion of priests and *castrati*. The music was excellent; but the last-mentioned unhappy creatures, although their science and taste were indisputable, all wore upon their countenances an air of the deepest dejection.

On the 16th of November, I once more quitted this peaceful sort of life for the more glorious but at the same time less convenient duties of military service, marching about five leagues to Mafra, to which place the road is paved with *basaltes*. Here is a very noble monastery erected in consequence of a vow made by one of the Portuguese monarchs, who had, during a fit of illness, sworn that he would convert the poorest monastery in the country into the richest.

The place itself is unimportant, and lies on the sea-shore; but the religious establishment in question is abundantly worth the observation of a stranger. It is situated upon a height, and comprises, within one large square, a church, a convent, and a palace. The roof of these buildings is flat; and it was said, that Marshal Junot, during his occupation of the place, mustered several thousand of his troops thereupon. The interior of the church is of the finest marble, but there is a deficiency of light.

Upon its walls are a variety of pictures by the most celebrated masters; but all these adornments were insufficient to preserve it from the rude appropriation of the military, from whom (particularly from the cavalry, who stabled their horses in different parts of the building) it sustained much damage. On the 18th I reached, after a tedious journey over muddy roads, the entrenchment at Torres Vedras, where I had expected to find my regiment, but was disappointed.

Chapter 22

French Deserters

On the 15th of the same month, Massena had retired from before Lord Wellington's entrenchment, and proceeded to Santarem. The difficulties which surrounded him, from want of provision, sickness among his troops, and other adventitious causes, compelled him to take this measure. On the discovery of the French Marshal's retrograde movement, Lord Wellington, without loss of time, commenced a pursuit; and that same day the advanced guard of the allies entered Alenquer, which had been the enemy's head-quarters. Hence it was, that on arriving at the lines, I found them partly vacated, and our regiment, amongst others, on the advance.

Alenquer, it was obvious, had been a pretty place, and situated in a fruitful country; but its spoliation during the period it was occupied by the French troops was dreadful in the extreme. It is scarcely to be expected that habits of cleanliness should obtain amongst a mass of rude soldiery; but really the French carried the contrary principle to an unexampled extent. The pollution of the houses at Alenquer was unnameable, almost inconceivable, and the destruction of the furniture altogether wanton—it is true, there was no great deal of this to destroy, for the Portuguese are not apt to overburthen their rooms with luxuries of even comforts; but it should seem that, for the sake of their own convenience, what accommodations they found should have been preserved by the invaders.

On the 21st I pursued my course towards Cartaxo, the road to which place was abundantly strewn with the carcases of horses, oxen, &c. mingled every here and there with dead bodies of the enemy. At Cartaxo, Lord Wellington had fixed his head-quarters, and it was consequently no easy matter to obtain lodgement—the rather as the French had practised here the same Vandalic system which I have hinted at in speaking of Alenquer. From Cartaxo, a distance of four leagues further enabled me to come up with the army, the left wing of which was actually engaged with the enemy, and from the adjacent high hills the scene of action was commanded, and both armies lay in full view. Towards afternoon, the firing ceased.

It was curious to observe the number of nuns, and other women of the country, who followed in the train of our army—thus violating that kind of reserve, and in fact (as relates to the former) that solemn oath which prohibited them from such contact. The monks, too, no longer revelling in the possession of rich acres and rosy wine, trailed along timidly and despondingly, as if hopeless of the least tranquillity except in the boisterous companionship of a large army.

The 16th of December, I marched with a party of the regiment from St. Joan de Ribeira, two leagues to Rio Mayor. The French, in their retreat, (whether actuated by vexation or in the mere spirit of wantonness, I know not,) had committed a thousand enormities unheard of in civilized warfare. Even the graves of the dead were not held sacred; and the bodies which had been quietly and hopefully committed to them, were exhumated and left to infest the surrounding atmosphere with their pestilential effluvia.

Hence, we were frequently obliged, from motives of security, to halt, and seek the breeze stimulated by a clump of trees, until the space before us had been cleared from heaps of these pernicious objects. Occasionally, encouraged by our presence, some of the inhabitants of the several villages returned to their abandoned dwelling-places, but fled again, with loud and desperate outcries, on perceiving the desolation and horror which had been introduced in and about their household asylums. The vintage and olive-harvest were altogether neglected. The fruits rotted upon the trees, or lay underneath in putrid masses. Many deserters almost daily came in from the enemy's camp, so gaunt, emaciated, and woebegone, that they scarcely retained the semblance of human beings—and telling a tale of distress and privation most afflicting to the compassionate hearer.

Thus did Massena, with his ruined and ghastly crew, continue, like a demon, to infest the country which his presence had blasted; and having taken up a strong position near Santarem, was suffered gradually to exhaust himself in its retention. From the haughty assailant, he had been reduced to the apprehensive fugitive; and in the hopes of receiving a reinforcement of troops and provisions from Spain, contrived to keep his ground till the beginning of March.

These hopes, however, were, as the event proved, fallacious; for his lines were completely environed by hostile parties of the allies, who, hovering round his position, effectually cut off all communication. On the other hand, the open country behind supplied us plentifully with every necessary, and the returning spring brought fresh troops from England, and revived, not only the face of Nature, but the health and spirits of our men.

On the preceding Christmas Day, a festival was given by the commanding-officer of our regiment which somewhat reminded me of the nuptials of a Saxon peasant; inasmuch, as every guest was required to bring, not only himself, but the chair he was to sit on, the plate he was to eat from, and the spoon which was to convey the soup into his mouth.

Even with these inconveniences, however, since there really was good cheer, our lot was comparatively excellent—many of the unfortunate country-people being altogether destitute of food, and in some instances, compelled by hard necessity to resort even to the grass of the field for insufficient and unwholesome nourishment.

Strict orders were issued carefully to preserve the wine-presses, which would have been irreplaceable if lost: the agricultural prospects for the ensuing year were, in fact, altogether mournful to a degree; for, under existing circumstances, no attention could be paid to the cultivation of the necessary crops,

On the 16th of January, 1811, I accompanied a division of my regiment, together with one of the 16th Light Dragoons, to Caldas. The road led us partly across barren hills and morasses towards the sea-shore. Upon our arrival in the afternoon, we found, in the market-place, a crowd of venders of fruit and bread. These people, upon our approach, mistaking us for French troops, took precipitate flight, abandoning their baskets to our mercy.

They soon however were undeceived, and lost no time in returning to claim compensation for their articles; and so prodigious was their complaisance, that they scrupled neither to welcome us into the deserted houses (wherein themselves were interlopers) nor to assist us in breaking open such as had been secured. The fugitives had left behind the greater part of their furniture, which, as the place had not fallen into the enemy's hands, was in tolerable plight: indeed, it was this circumstance which had occasioned our present visit, since it was most desirable that any place which had hitherto escaped should be kept free from the spoliation of the enemy.

Caldas is remarkable on account of its sulphurous springs, which are numerous and powerful. Over them is constructed a handsome bathing-house, wherein four baths are included, close to the springs, and hence the vapour is condensed and retained. These medicinal baths have, in fact, wholly constituted the prosperity of the town, and occasioned the erection of many elegant houses, and also of a royal palace, with an extensive park in which are several ponds filled with gold and silver fish.

In a saloon adjoining the baths, and, appropriated to the company as a promenade, is represented, (by way, I suppose, of exciting lively and agreeable ideas in the minds of the invalids,) an *auto-da-fé* in all its ingenious and amusing details, the figures of the size of life. Close by is a chapel,—its entrance ornamented with a choice collection of crutches, respectively deposited by cripples who had recovered the use of their limbs from bathing in the waters of Caldas.

In this place we continued until the beginning of February, on the 4th day of which we experienced a smart shock of an earthquake, which at a distance of about four leagues, at Penicho, (whose situation is semi-insular,) was felt very severely indeed. Our patrols extended their reconnaissance as far as a large monastery in the neighbourhood of Caldas which had been wantonly fired by order of Massena; and the Catholic Frenchmen had, in indecent mockery, ranged the various images belonging to the church as sentries around its ruins!

On the 8th inst. the division of the legion returned to Rio Mayor, leaving the English detachment alone in Caldas, as it was thought quite sufficient for the exclusion of the enemy's foraging parties. I found my former quarters at Rio Mayor in very bad condition; a strong corps of French, under Junot, having the day before made a sudden inroad, and after committing every possible species of devastation, retired again. This irruption had been undertaken in order to penetrate to the neighbouring salt-works, and was productive to Marshal Junot of a wound in his nose, which was perforated by a ball from one of our hussars.

For several successive nights, these interruptions were repeated, but without any particular effect. At length they ceased; and meanwhile, prisoners and deserters came in more numerously than ever, Massena had succeeded in obtaining a reinforcement; but this, instead of rendering his condition better, only served (from the scarcity of provisions) to make it worse. About the middle of February, the croaking of the frogs announced the approach of spring: the fruit-trees began to blossom, and, had it not been for that constitutional listlessness peculiar to the Portuguese, their circumstances might hereby have been much ameliorated. Our stay in Rio Mayor extended to the early part of March, when Massena broke up from his position, and resumed his retreat. It had been latterly with him as with a dying man:—almost every hour appeared to produce a diminution of strength. On his departure, our regiment received orders to hold itself in constant readiness for pursuit.

CHAPTER 23

Orders to Return to England

On the night between the 5th and 6th of March, finally commenced the retreat of Marshal Massena, with his army, from the Portuguese territory. Our troops pursued him at his very heels into the heart of Spain—accomplishing a distance of seventy-five leagues in twenty-eight days, which, for so great a body of men, was no slight exertion, particularly as we were frequently obliged to halt, in order to await the arrival of provisions.

Hence, the forces were occasionally reduced to the very extremity of fatigue: and the exhaustion of the enemy might be inferred from our own, with the addition on his part of absence of supplies. In the course of this march, we were continually victors, whenever engaged; and these affairs recurred pretty often, from the desire of the enemy to keep us at bay.

The retreat of the French was attended with every atrocity which the mind can conceive. Smoking villages, wasted fields, dilapidated towns, conspired alternately to attest their rage, disappointment, and fiendish barbarity. Nor were these ravages confined to inanimate objects. Slaughter as well as fire was enlisted into his service by the fugitive *soi-disant* king of Portugal.

Youth and age were found lying together wounded in ditches, or upon the high road; and mingling their cries with those of the sick enemy, who had been abandoned to their fate. Herds of unoffending beasts were included in the work of destruction, and clogged the paths, mixing their death-groans with the sighs of their human fellow-sufferers, whom the diabolical foe, having, in many instances, stricken to the earth, had plundered of their garments, and left exposed to nakedness as well as suffering. An eye-witness of the barbarities perpetrated in Santarem, during its occupation by Massena, assured me as a fact, among other instances, that the soldiers had strung up twelve old men, in the cloisters of one of the monasteries, to represent, as they said, the twelve apostles! They stuck human heads upon poles, as marks to shoot at; and the fate of nine unfortunate nuns, who fell into the power of these monsters, is really too horrible to contemplate.

On the 7th of March, we broke up from our bivouac, and marched over bad roads four leagues to Torres Novas. In front of a village, which had been burned by the French, we found a suckling infant, in a basket lying near the road, beside a fire which had probably been lighted by the enemy.

As our march proceeded, the instances which I have already detailed of the enemy's cruelty were manifested afresh at almost every step. The town of Leiria, which had suffered immensely, was burning through the space of eleven days; and in all quarters were groups of butchered or mangled brutes; some with their heads twisted backwards, others hamstrung, or mutilated in various ways.

Early on the morning of the 11th instant, our advanced guard, which had been reinforced by several corps of heavy cavalry as well as some infantry regiments, broke up for the purpose of attacking the enemy, who had posted himself securely at Pombal. The road being dry and good, our horse-troops and artillery set forward at a brisk trot, and the foot-soldiers in quick march. To facilitate the progress of the latter, their knapsacks were entrusted to the charge of the heavy dragoons.

At this rate did we journey along the high road leading from Lisbon to Oporto, above a league, and the very earth seemed to vibrate under the multitudinous tramp of the warriors. In the afternoon, we arrived at Pombal, where we found the enemy, to the number of about 20,000, drawn up in battle array. They had fortified the old castle, in hopes of retaining the place, but to little purpose, as they were speedily forced from it. Towards evening, we bivouacked on this side the town, whilst the French occupied the other; and the respective watchfires were so close, that, at a small distance, they appeared as if actually confounded together.

On the 12th instant, we resumed our march, passing through the town, which presented the effects of an almost universal conflagration; and beyond, at the gorge of a narrow defile, in the direction of Redinha, the French corps was planted upon a height. Here they were attacked by Lord Wellington himself, and dislodged; the cannonading was kept up for several hours. The light cavalry was to have pursued the foe; but, in consequence of there being only one bridge, and that very narrow, across the river Redinha, this plan was necessarily abandoned.

We, therefore, retired a little, and took up our quarters for the night in the vicinity of Condeixa, whither we marched on the following day, and which we found, in common with the other towns on our route, blazing and deserted. Behind this place the enemy had selected a very strong position, from which, on account of the burning state of the town, he could not be easily removed. A division of infantry, however, under General Picton, succeeded in turning his left flank and ultimately in dislodging him.

On the 14th of March, the fire in Condeixa having subsided, and the enemy completely abandoned the place, we entered it The French general seems to have intended, by defending this post so strongly, to secure his retreat to Coimbra; but, owing to the activity and good conduct of the Portuguese militia by whom Coimbra was garrisoned, and who had blown up the middle arch of the bridge and fortified the place,—together with the rapid advance of Lord Wellington,—this design was altogether frustrated, and the upper part of the province of Beira consequently rescued from hostile fire and sword.

We pursued our course to the Ponto de Murcella, where the enemy again presented himself; the mountainous region yielding him considerable advantage, it behoved the allied generals to attack him in greater force, and he was successively driven, though in good order, from one height to another. As night approached we bivouacked not far from the Ponto de Murcella, and found ourselves, on account of the cold, obliged to set fire to the olive-trees which surrounded us.

On the 15th we commenced our march, at midday, and passed over several high hills to the little town of Miranda de Corvo. The road was actually clogged with various articles, (including coaches, wagons, &c.) which the enemy, in his quick retreat, had found it impossible to carry off. In addition to these encumbrances, others of a far more melancholy character were not wanting—numerous dead and dying, both of friendly Portuguese, and of foes, lining the pathway.

On the 16th, we once more came up with the enemy, who had collected almost his whole force near the river Ceira, where he was attacked by several divisions of our infantry. The brigade with which I was had been posted upon a height, and remained peaceful spectators, as the cavalry could not of course be used in so mountainous a country. The firing continued till late in the night, when the French were compelled to retreat in the greatest disorder.

We bivouacked close to the field of battle, in a forest, during very heavy rain and in utter darkness, which indeed was so dense as to occasion abundant accidents, though not, generally speaking, of a very serious nature. Many ludicrous scenes, in fact, occurred, on the men seeking each an unoccupied tree under which to ensconce himself; and midnight had long passed before anything like silence or repose was obtained.

Next day a thick fog followed the heavy rain, and prevented the army from making progress until afternoon, as it was impossible sooner to discover which direction the enemy had taken. We then proceeded across the field of battle to the narrow pass through which the enemy had been driven, and found the bridge of Ceira blown up, and that river so swollen by the rains as to be scarcely fordable.

On the 18th instant we broke up at ten o'clock a. m. and

proceeded a league, to the bridge of Murcella, which crosses the Elva. Here our battalion came up with the main army, which was collected upon a hill this side the bridge, whence the enemy were perceptible on the other side, withdrawing themselves. It was, however, impracticable to pursue them closely, as the bridge itself was strongly held, as was likewise the long defile adjacent we were therefore compelled to remain and quiescently witness his retreat.

On the 19th, before daybreak, we commenced our march, in order to arrive in good time at the river Elva, the bridge over which having been destroyed, a temporary wooden one had been constructed for the use of the infantry, whilst the cavalry and artillery were obliged to ford the stream. When our brigade had effected its passage, it waited until a sufficient number of infantry had crossed, and then continuing its march, made upwards of six hundred prisoners.

During the whole of this march every possible care and precaution was taken by the English authorities and commander-in-chief respecting accommodations for the sick and wounded. To each division was attached a certain number of covered cars so contrived as to admit of about twelve men each, and, as they hung upon springs, the invalids were secured from jarring motion as well as from wet:—upon these abominable roads, it is true, there was always some chance of an overthrow—and, instead of two horses, which would have sufficed upon a decent highway, eight were absolutely necessary for every car.

On the 21st instant we met, on our way, with a wounded Frenchman, who was lying amongst the bushes where he was exposed to the imminent hazard of death from privation and cold. Several others were lying scattered around quite dead, and who had probably been despatched by the clubs of some erratic parties of Portuguese. I procured this poor fellow some articles of clothing (of which he had been entirely stripped) and had him conveyed into one of the cars, for which act of service I received the warmest acknowledgements.

At length we arrived at Coimbra, which we found in a very

mournful and desolate state, and here I remained three days, at the expiration of which I proceeded with my party, and came to a village in the neighbourhood of Ponte do Murcella, where, however, not a single human being was to be met with, and where I took up my quarters in a half-burnt house. Of dead bodies there were plenty, as the air, for a considerable space round about, bore ample testimony.

At Penances, the deeds of darkness and spoliation which had thus far marked the enemy's retreat were terminated; as Lord Wellington had signified to the French commander, that if any farther devastation or firing either of town or village should be practised, he would no longer interpose his authority and protection between the French prisoners and the enraged Portuguese. In consequence of this, the houses, at any rate, had been left standing in Penances.

On the 30th instant, we arrived at Celerico where Lord Wellington had his head-quarters. The English army was here collected in order to force the enemy from his strong position near Guarda, which however he abandoned without a struggle and retreated upon Sabugal, on the shore of the Coa.

The course of the campaign led us to Guinaldo, where we remained in security until the 2nd of May, on which day we broke up, as the whole allied army was fast concentrating itself and we anticipated a battle. Early in the morning, sundry Spanish fugitives arrived in our camp, reporting the advance of the enemy from Rodrigo, in considerable force, whereupon we retired upon Espaja. Lord Wellington, however, in full expectation of a favourable result, left a squadron behind in Guinaldo, which subsequently, in conjunction with the light Spanish cavalry, commanded by Don Julian Sanchez, rendered great service by annoying the rear of the hostile force.

We marched to Espaja by circuitous routes, not knowing but the French might be preceding us, and when, in the dusk of evening, we arrived near that place, a party, with an officer at its head, was despatched to ascertain this fact, the reality of which was confirmed by their report. We therefore turned into the road leading to Fuentes D'Onore, where we arrived at midnight. In this place, we found a number of light infantry, and bivouacked upon ploughed ground. After a few hours rest we put ourselves again in motion, and joined some other cavalry regiments at Espaja, which we reached by crossing a plain, and where these regiments were already engaged with the enemy, whilst the commander-in-chief, from a height occupied by him and overlooking the scene of action, saw the advance of the main French army across the small river Azava, a circumstance which was announced to the troops by loud signals.

His Lordship having obtained the object he had in view, the army returned to Fuentes, before which place the light infantry was drawn up in battle array; but they being opposed by a very superior force were obliged to give way and retreat. The enemy thus possessed himself of Fuentes, which however he was not able to maintain, as a Scottish regiment, which had been sent to the support of the infantry, retook it by storm, and in their possession it remained the following night.

On the 4th instant, which was the first day of the battle of Fuentes D'Onore, scarcely had morning dawned when our slumbers upon the stony ground were interrupted by a heavy firing, which arose from the enemy making another desperate attack upon that town, whereby our infantry were forced, though but for a few brief moments, to evacuate the place. In the course of the day, this assault was renewed, with no better success; immense loss, however, ensued on both sides.

Towards noon, the fire slackened against us, in the centre, and was directed upon the right wing, whither, in consequence, our light cavalry, together with the mounted artillery, received orders to repair. The 16th Dragoon Regiment with the Hussar Regiment of the Legion were posted close to Nove D'Avare; here the hostile cavalry were so near, that we could plainly observe their movements; but as they seemed perfectly quiet.

I joined some of my comrades in making preparations for cooking, as we had hardly touched: a morsel daring the last two days. The outposts having been duly stationed, we bivouacked under oak trees upon fragrant grass; but day had not yet appeared when the signal for rising was given, and the two light cavalry brigades were immediately drawn up and marched against the enemy's cavalry—the right wing of which was considerably increased in numerical strength.

On gaining the opposite shore of the petty river Duas Caras, (where the hostile cavalry was posted,) our troops halted, and our regiment and a squadron of the 16th were directed to proceed to attack. It was here hard work for the horses to scale the steep heights, and when they had succeeded in doing so, a murderous conflict was commenced—in which the 16th, having reached the point rather earlier than the rest, took the largest share. It was vain, however, to coin tend against greatly superior force, and it was at length found necessary to fall back upon the centre of the main army at Fuentes, which movement was accomplished in the best possible order.

Immediately after, the enemy fell upon our infantry, but were met with such an effective fire by the English sharpshooters and the Brunswickers, (who had lain concealed,) that they retreated with precipitate haste and in great confusion. Not satisfied, however, with these successive attempts, the French made another and a most desperate one from their centre upon Fuentes D'Onore, which lasted several hours. Many of our brave fellows were hewn down every minute, and the wounded were immediately borne to a hillock in the rear which was defended by a brigade of light cavalry, and where all the medical staff attached to the army was accumulated.

These attacks, indeed, continued, with very little intermission, until late in the afternoon; varying in their severity from one wing to the other, but aimed more particularly against Fuentes. I was despatched, towards evening, to Castlebomb, nearly a league from the field of battle, where with great difficulty shelter could be found for the wounded officers,, the French having left the usual devastating marks of their presence. The lower part of the houses were turned into stables.

Amongst others who were conducted here, was an English

officer of the 16th Dragoons, who assured me (his wound thoroughly corroborating his assertion) that from the place where he had received his hurt for upwards of a mile he had carried on horseback, in the upper part of his thigh, the shot of a three-pounder, not being able sooner to meet with a surgeon capable of extracting it!

This unfortunate gentleman, however, died the following day, almost while in the act of undergoing the necessary amputation. Another, who was less severely wounded, was brother to the celebrated Spanish general, Don Julian Sanchez. Both of these brothers had sworn eternal hatred and vengeance against the French, by whose instrumentality they had lost their parents and their sister. Not long before, the one who was here wounded, had with a party of guerillas been to his father's house; and found quartered there a French colonel, who had been accessory to the murder of his relations. Upon this man, Sanchez of course took dire vengeance, after reproaching him in no measured terms with his unmanly atrocity.

On the following day, I heard a curious instance of Lord Wellington's personal activity. On the day after the principal conflict at Fuentes, he received information that Marshal Soult was pressing forward against the English *corps d'armée* in the south near Badajoz, upon which his lordship started instantly from the field of battle in order to be there before any attack was made. In the course of this hurried journey, he rode two horses dead, notwithstanding relays had been constantly in readiness; and at one point, took a stream which was so deep and impetuous that two dragoons, who accompanied him, sank and were drowned. The victorious general, however, by virtue either of his better horse or better luck, got safely over and accomplished the distance in an incredibly short space of time.

Travelling on with the wounded, I, on the 12th of May, again reached Celerico, which place was in a most deplorable state. No accommodation whatever was procurable for the unfortunate sufferers, and even a little clean straw was considered a luxury within the reach of comparatively few, even among the officers themselves. I cannot help smiling on recollection of a warm dispute I once held with a man who claimed the right and title to an old broken chair which I was desirous to procure for one of the invalids!

At Celerico we remained until the 7th of June, when we proceeded to Coimbra, through Villa Cortes, Vinho, and other places,—the country being of the most lovely description, even amidst the ravages which had resulted from a state of warfare.

Amongst other evils springing from that prolific source, was the blow given to commendable, if not religious feeling, by the demolition of the monasteries and convents. These receptacles of tranquillity and of apparent devotion were now almost universally converted into stables or hospitals, and their peaceful inhabitants replaced by boisterous soldiery.

Even timid nuns, the rules of whose order had prohibited them from wandering beyond the extent of the convent garden, and who rarely saw a human being save their fellow-recluses or their confessor, were frequently to be met with in the ranks of the English army, performing the most menial offices for soldiers and heretics! The libraries of the monasteries were, I am sorry to add, seldom respected, but committed by wholesale to the flames or to some other method of destruction. The troops of "*mendicant* friars" were enlarged beyond all conception—and they had become snob not from voluntary dedication to the rules of that class, but from a more imperative principle—necessity.

A great number of Portuguese boys, from twelve to eighteen years of age, attached themselves to the English officers and others, giving their services for an almost nominal gratuity—and forgetting, in the adoption of the customs of their Protestant masters, those regulations of the Catholic church which had been impressed upon their childhood. What effect this circumstance may have (if any) on their future opinions, time will show.

I have in various parts of this narrative lamented the wanton destruction of Portuguese and Spanish property. I really, however, am disposed to wish that the table whereon I now write had shared some such fate; for it seems to have survived so many centuries, and is grown so intolerably shattered and unsteady, that I can scarce frame a single letter, and in taking my meals am necessitated to use the utmost caution to prevent the overthrow, of the dishes.

During my stay at Coimbra, which extended to the 20th of June, I received an intimation that my appointment in the Legion was changed from the cavalry to the infantry, and accordingly had to procure certain necessary equipments. The chief body of our German infantry had been removed from the northern to the southern *corps d'armée,* and to the post of the latter it became incumbent on me to proceed.

My road for this purpose lay through the desolate province Beira, across a portion, of the Estrella chain of mountains, and through part of the province Alentejo to the frontiers of Estremadura. Before I left Coimbra, several trades people had visited that city, from Oporto and Lisbon, bringing with them a large stock of goods, which they sold at exorbitantly high prices, knowing that abundance of the English officers were dreadfully in want of articles, of clothing. Through one of these worthies I supplied myself both with garments and provisions for several months; and having done so, commenced my march with my domestic servant and a few privates.

I had now to retrace the route I had so recently traversed. On our arrival near our journey's end, I was given to understand, much to my surprise, that the battalion I was about to join had received orders to return to England. Immediately on hearing this, I hastened forward to ascertain its truth, and on reaching the encampment, discovered that the officers, non-commissioned officers, and band of the 7th Battalion were actually about to return to England, in order to be completed, whilst the privates were grafted into the four other battalions of the Legion stationed in the Peninsula, and which had hitherto served with the first division of the British army.

They were now lying encamped at Santa Olalla, near Badajoz, which latter fortress had been for some weeks blockaded, but had been relieved by the advance of the enemy's force under Soult.

Chapter 24

Voyage to England

On the 4th of July, 1811, the battalion quitted the seat of war in Portugal, and commenced its march towards Lisbon. Our route lay through the province of Alentejo, across a country consisting, for the greater part, of barren deserts, strewn here and there with clumps of turpentine-trees.

On the seventh day we reached Abrantes, where we halted two days, and then proceeded in boats down the Tagus to the capital; our horses being committed to the care of people who conducted them by land. The smaller craft made very rapid way; but as I was unfortunately a passenger in one of the larger vessels, I had to put up with much dilatoriness and delay; and, on one occasion, our people toiled so near the shore that the rigging got entangled in some branches of trees, and hence a total stop was put to our progress for the present.

We compelled, however, a boat which followed to take us in, and hereby were enabled to proceed some distance farther; but the boatmen soon manifesting unequivocal signs of fatigue, we found it vain to speculate on reaching Santarem (as had been our intention) and were obliged to halt for the night at a lone house on the left shore of the Tagus.

On the following morning we returned our passage, and on arriving at Santarem were accommodated with another vessel, which making rather brisker sail brought as, towards afternoon, to the Tajo Novo, where we again changed our boat for a larger, (which the increased depth and width of the river allowed in to do,) and next day I once more landed at the fish-market of Lisbon.

In the Portuguese metropolis I remained this time six days, at the expiration of which, after having bade farewell, in common with my brother-officers, (over a bottle or two of excellent Vittoria wine,) to this priest and war ridden country, I put off, in the evening, to find my transport-ship, which was lying among a number of others in the mouth of the Tagus. The discovery of the right vessel, however, proved no easy matter, on account of the darkness and the stormy weather, added to the multiplicity of all kinds of ships at anchor.

At length, in despair, I made the boatmen put me on board the best-looking transport in our vicinity, wherein I passed the night, and the next morning enabled me to transfer myself to my appointed vessel. Having remained here stationary till the 22nd instant in the immediate neighbourhood of Fort St. Julian, which defends the entrance of the Tagus, a signal was at length given to weigh anchor at daybreak, and by seven o'clock we were in full sail,

The squadron amounted to about thirty vessels—chiefly consisting of empty transports, which had brought troops and military stores from England hither. Under the influence of contrary north-west winds, we beat about some time though without sustaining any damage, and passed the Baora, as certain sunken sand-banks are denominated at the efflux of the Tagus, and by which the navigation of the place is rendered in a degree dangerous.

The wind, as I have said, was completely adverse, but as our orders for sailing were peremptory, we were compelled to steer westward, and by midday had lost sight of land, a circumstance which would not have occurred had the wind been favourable, in which case, we should have kept sight of the Portuguese shore for several days.

On the following morning, the wind grew more violent; we therefore drove still further to westward instead of to north-east, and hence a long voyage was in prospect. Notwithstanding this stiff breeze, however, and the quick sailing on our part, I did not find the motion of the ship very disagreeable—perhaps my former experience had seasoned me a little to the pranks of the ocean.

On the 24th and 25th the wind slackened, and on the 26th we were quite becalmed, and continued so during the space of two days, although the swell was still uncommonly heavy. During this interval, I passed into another vessel, a passage, by the by, of no gentle kind, as it took several stout men half an hour to accomplish it, so rough was the sea.

On the 29th the wind sprang up again, though still unfavourable, and blew us in the direction of America, which continent we really seemed as if about to take in our way. The 31st we descried a huge body floating near us, which upon being hauled aboard, proved to be a block, of American timber of large proportions, and whereon thousands of *polypi* had fastened themselves—so that the entire mass seemed instinct with life. Most of these animals were from four to six inches in length.

On the 1st of August, things looked more agreeably. We had a smart breeze from the south, which, had it struck up at the time we issued from the Tagus, would have served our purpose admirably: in present circumstances, however, we could only avail ourselves of it as a side-wind. On the 3rd instant, our enemy from the north-east obtruded himself again to obstruct our progress, and we had consequently the agreeable prospect of beating about in the Atlantic for the space of perhaps two or three months!—an event by no means uncommon in this short voyage; owing to the prevalence, in summer, of north and west winds.

At length I heard, on the morning of the 4th whilst still in my hammock, the glad tidings of the wind having veered into the right quarter, and, as it so continued, the captain of our convoy-ship planted, a few days after, a little fête on board his vessel, for the celebration of which he requested the assistance of our band, at the same time inviting the officers of the Legion, and specifying, by way of temptation, that he had several ladies on board, who had consented to honour the party by joining in a dance.

The notion of a ball held out at sea, in a ball-room which was tossing about in the Atlantic, amused me a good deal, and I anticipated no small gratification from the novelty of the thing:—we were, however, disappointed, on account of the increased turbulence of the breeze, and obliged to content ourselves (in which to speak truth we found no difficulty) with viewing once more the shores of England, which we neared rapidly, and found ourselves coasting along in the British Channel on the 11th instant. Next morning, we ran through the Needles, and entered the harbour of Portsmouth, after a passage of twenty days, during which we were quite out of sight of land. No sooner had we cast anchor, than I, with several other officers, proceeded on shore, and quartered ourselves in the principal inn of this important seaport.

Thus terminated this little voyage, which, although toilsome in some respects, was not altogether disagreeable, since we had no storms, and were enabled, owing to the fine weather, to be a good deal on deck, and what is still better, to eat our meals and discuss our wine without the intervention of an unceremonious lurch.

In Portsmouth I remained but a few days, and having procured leave of absence, started for the metropolis, which I reached early on a fine autumnal morning. It is scarcely possible to conceive the feelings induced in me by the contrast which the face of abundance and uniform comfort diffused around, presented to the abandoned, half-burnt and half-ruined country of Portugal.

The Portuguese, in fact, even when unannoyed by the causes which had latterly conspired to depress them, seem unfitted, from their indolent and careless habits, to profit by the luxurious soil on which they live, and which might suffice to render their country one of the finest under the face of the sun—whilst, on the other hand, in England, and more particularly in and round the capital, everything is activity, life, and enterprise. Of every advantage the people possess they seem disposed to make the most, and their quick step and earnest look bespeak that the mind participates in the energy of the body.

After eight days' stay in London, which soon flitted by, in the midst of business and pleasure, I repaired to Bexhill, the point of rendezvous for our battalion. This town is sixty-five miles distant from London, on the sea-coast, in the county of Sussex. Until of late years, it was a very inconsiderable place indeed, consisting of a few houses only; and owes its present advancement to the dignity of a market-town to the French threats of invasion, which occasioned several barracks to be constructed here, as a point well calculated for the station of a numerous body of troops.

The extraordinary heat of this year (1811), celebrated as the "comet-year," which relaxed not until the month of October, actually made me believe that I was still in Portugal, and rendered me anxious for the approach of winter, which found us still at Bexhill until the 12th of December, when orders arrived for us to hold ourselves in readiness to proceed once more to Portsmouth in order to embark thence for Sicily.

Our battalion had, by this, increased to 800 men, in consequence of the incorporation of numerous French deserters. This reinforcement was, in truth, necessary, since the English were now so completely blocked out from Germany that it was impracticable to obtain recruits from the natural source—Hanover. But it is inconceivable how much trouble was incurred in teaching these men the exercise, since they knew scarcely one word of German, and still less, if possible, of English.

According to these instructions, therefore, the troops left Bexhill; the 1st division on the 16th December; and the two others on the two ensuing days. The march to Portsmouth occupied his days, over fine smooth reads rearing along the coast by Lewes, Brighton, Shoreham, (where we halted on Christmas Day,) and across by Arundel and Chichester. No sooner had we arrived at the port, than the men were at once embarked. Several matters of business, both private and professional, induced my continuance on shore a day or two longer, but I was necessitated to expedite them, as it was determined, should the wind serve, that we should sail on the 1st of January.

Three transport-ships contained the whole of our battalion, and on the largest of these three vessels I was accommodated. It was nearly of the size of a frigate, and had formerly been a French *corvette*. It was now pretty well stocked, as (including the entire ship's company) there were 500 souls aboard.

However much a matter of course our embarkation might be, the making way was by no means equally so; contrary winds, indeed, prevailed for the space of two months, during which we lay at anchor in the reads of Spithead. The monotony of this condition was unutterable, more especially as, owing to the almost hourly chance of our getting under weigh, it was difficult to obtain permission to go ashore; hence, the least circumstance which occurred to break this chain of dullness was eagerly caught hold of by us, and we took occasion of the queen's birthday, to hold a little fête, hoist our various colours from the mast-heads, and fire a *feu-de-joie,* which was answered by the adjacent batteries.

Another occurrence which created some excitement, although of no very lively character, was the execution of two sailors for murder, whilst a third was, in the midst of uncommonly stormy weather, visited with a considerable number of ladies on board each ship, in the presence of the whole of the crews, who were all mustered for the occasion.

On the 1st of March, a fresh easterly wind arose, by virtue of which we hoped to have a quick passage to our destination; but this was fallacious, as we were obliged, on account of its veering again, to anchor at Falmouth; at length, it once more blew favourably, and on the 13th inst. we ware in sight of Cape Finisterre. From hence we sailed on to Gibraltar, at which place we arrived on the 17th, rather behind the rest of the fleet, which had been augmented in various ways to a great extent.

However desirous I was to take a personal survey of this celebrated rock, and the city built upon it, I found it impracticable, as signals: were flying on board the commodore's ship for making further way. Judging, indeed, by what I could perceive from on board,. I lost little, as nothing can be more uninteresting than the aspect of Gibraltar, for the possession of which so many battles have been fought and so many lives lost. Sterile and precipitous it rises from the ocean, and scarcely does the eye, in wandering over it, encounter the least object of a verdant nature.

Upon the highest points are posted sentry-boxes and telegraphs, and on the middle and loftiest summit are to be found a number of monkeys (from which circumstance the height is denominated Ape Hill): these animals are, in common with their tribe generally, very mischievous and abominable thieves, often penetrating at night into the soldiers' quarters, and stealing the bread and other provisions; still, however, they are not suffered to be destroyed, it being said that they once by their vigilance contributed mainly to the assistance of the garrison whilst in a state of siege.

The town, as is well known, lies at the foot of these precipitous heights, by which it is sheltered, alas, too completely, from the east and north-east winds; for, in consequence, when these winds have, for any length of time, prevailed, yellow fever and other disorders follow in their train. The harbour and roads are, on the other hand, so utterly exposed to the operation of the south and south-west winds, that they become hazardous to the shipping, and vessels are frequently stranded, which misfortune befell several of our fleet.

By help of a glass I could discern sundry fine and spacious ranges of building, adorned in front with trees and in some instances with gardens, and among these the governor's house and that of the commissary-general were conspicuous, and are held to be particularly deserving of admiration on account of the skill displayed in the laying-out of grounds on so rocky a soil. The naked eye could likewise command, from the deck, the large town of Algesiras and various smaller towns; and, besides, the African fortifications of Ceuta, presenting altogether a prospect interesting and magnificent in the highest degree.

On the third morning after our arrival, we again got under weigh; and although many of our ships (such for instance as were bound to the East and West Indies, Portugal, &c.) had meanwhile parted company, our numbers were replenished by the accession of numerous Turkish, Greek, and Spanish vessels, which, from their peculiar build, rigging, &c. were far behind the tight English sailors.

For the first two days we kept both shores in view; on the third, the African coast alone was visible; and on the 22nd inst. land had disappeared altogether. Next day we could descry in the distance the Algerine hills, and a dead calm ensued, which gave our seamen opportunity to catch several turtles, weighing each from twenty to thirty pounds. These fish, in consequence of the calm, floated on the surface of the water, basking and apparently dozing in the warm rays of the sun, and becoming consequently an easy prey to our men, who fairly hauled them by the feet into the boats wherein they had cautiously approached the spots where the turtles lay.

On the 25th of March, the wind springing up favourably, we sailed past the island of Sardinia, and two days after, that of Sicily, proceeding onwards to Malta, which, together with the island of Gozo, rose upon our view on the 30th instant.

Chapter 25

Entrance into Malta Harbour

On nearing Malta we were once more becalmed for awhile, a circumstance which enabled me to take a thorough view of this rock-island, if I may so express myself; but a little breeze freshening towards night, we glided the following morning into the harbour. Just as our numerous fleet was running in (to gaze upon which an immense number of spectators had assembled upon the heights around) the captured French ship, *Rivoli*, manned by its victors, together with an English line-of-battle ship and a frigate, sailed majestically after us; and it will readily be imagined that this occurrence afforded fresh stimulus to the enthusiastic lookers-on. Scarcely indeed had the admiral's flag-ship lying here, and the batteries, replied to our commodore's greeting, before a salvo, thrice-repeated, from all the vessels, and emulated by loud huzzas from the crews and the spectators on shore, fairly made the air vibrate, and produced a splendid effect, which I am really unable to describe. The *Rivoli* was of 84 guns, and had sailed quite new only a few days previously to her capture, from an Italian port

Having duly performed quarantine, we disembarked, contrary to expectation, on the 2nd of April, as Messina, the former capital of Sicily, (whither we were bound,) was understood to be already too full of troops, an expedition being about this time contemplated for Spain. Our quarters were established in the Fort Ricasoli, which lies on the left of the harbour-entrance, and is the coolest spot upon the whole island. It was difficult, by the by, to effect a landing, for the waves were running very high, and the water deep even at the point of springing ashore. From the shore a narrow path leads to the principal entrance of the fort, which is provided with a drawbridge and double gate.

Above the archway is a fine massy edifice, serving as the residence of the commandant, and all the buildings appropriated to the garrison are so constructed as to be proof against bombs or other hostile missiles. The rocks whereon this fort is erected are eternally washed by the sea, which in boisterous weather dashes against the batteries, and in some instances even over the whole fort. Towards the south-east is situated the yet stronger fortification of Vittoriosa, so called from the heroic defence it made against the Turks in the year 1565. It is reached by a long subterraneous passage excavated in the rock, and adjoins one of the eight towns of the island, namely, Citta Vittoriosa, or Il Borgo.

The day after our arrival the officers of our battalion received an invitation from those of a Sicilian regiment in English pay (and wherein were several English officers) to dinner. This regiment lay in Fort Vittoriosa; and as that fortress was more conveniently reached by water than by the subterraneous passage already alluded to, we proceeded thither in boats.

Our brother officers really treated us sumptuously: the saloon in which we dined was. of noble proportions: a table laid for seventy persons took up no more than one-half of its circumference, and was literally crowded with dainties of all descriptions, including the most costly wines. Pleasure and hilarity reigned supreme.

La Valette, formerly the residence of the Grand Master, but now of the British Governor, lies upon the right shore of the entrance into the principal harbour. The houses of this town, which is of tolerable size, are massively built, and there are amongst them many important-looking structures. In the streets are to be seen people of almost every nation;—some walking, some lounging about, and others, in the true oriental style, sitting cross-legged and very composedly smoking their *hookahs*.

The followers of this latter custom are chiefly occupied, if occupation it can be called, in the sale of various *bagatelles,* such as figs, tobacco, oils, &c. The curious speculator may here take, occasion to observe the characteristic differences between the European, Asiatic, African, and American races, which are presented to the eye almost at a single glance, as if on a card of living specimens. The Maltese himself, although it is fair to rank him with Europeans, approaches closely to the African in the contour of his features.

Amongst the public buildings is particularly distinguished the palace of government, (in other days of the Grand Master,) which stands in the centre of town, nearly upon the highest ground, and is square in its form, with five large gates. The grand staircase in this palace is one of the finest things of the kind I ever saw; nor is that the only object it contains worthy notice.

One of the saloons is decorated with portraits of the Bourbon family, of the size of life, and another is hung with the most splendid Gobelin tapestry, whilst a third contains portraits of the most distinguished Knights of the Order of Malta. The whole structure has a flat roof, with an elegant balustrade, and from which may be commanded a prospect truly magnificent both for character and extent. In front of the palace is a large open square, ornamented by a remarkable fountain, constructed in the seventeenth century by the then Grand Master.

The principal and most beautiful church in the town is that of St. John, in which are combined at once costliness, elegance, and science. On entering, the first object which strikes the visitor is the ceiling, which is covered with paintings of the knight Preri (better known under the name of Calabresen): the subjects are religious, and are executed with great ability. The walls are in some parts richly gilded, and in others covered with Gobelin tapestry, likewise worked with scripture-subjects. The floor is not less costly; being covered with memorial-stones, in Mosaic and coloured marble, of the several knights buried underneath.

The high altar consists of crimson porphyry, and another is encompassed with a railing of massive silver five feet high. The Emperor Napoleon, during his brief stay here, (when General

Bonaparte, and bound on the expedition to Egypt,) is said to have despoiled this church of property to a very great amount: but it is still the depository of incredible riches.

The productions of the island of Malta consist principally of wheat, Turkish corn, the finest southern fruits, (including the beautiful blood-orange,) and cotton. Thus, its produce fully supports its population, although the latter is somewhat redundant for the size of the place, amounting to about 100,000 souls. The soil was nevertheless originally very rocky and sterile, but was furnished by the enterprising knights with strata of earth from Sicily.

In no harbour could the shipping be more numerous and active than here. Not a day passed but was signalized by either the arrival or departure of vessels;—not a week but some large fleet, amounting to fifty or sixty sail, entered or quitted the harbour, and in either case,, the thunder of cannon announced the event. In fact, no place can be better fitted for purposes of commerce, partly owing to its advantageous situation and partly to the liberty which is enjoyed here both by the stranger and native. Smuggling is carried on in all directions:—no one pays taxes to England, and the only impost is for the purpose of keeping the roads and churches in good order.

The harbour and fortifications are kept in repair by the English government, and are consequently always in the best possible state. The batteries are constructed in the most durable way, and being whitewashed reflect strongly the rays of the sun—so much so, indeed, that from this cause, added to the sand-stone dust, ophthalmia is very prevalent upon the island.

The climate of Malta is one of the sultriest in Europe, and, at the end of June, 1812, the thermometer stood from 80 to 88 degrees Fahrenheit. The nights cool the air a little, and in the day the inhabitants sprinkle their houses liberally in order to allay the fervent heat. In August and September, however, relief no longer accrues from the night-time, and the glow is said to be almost intolerable. In April and the early part of May we had this year violent showers of rain and rather chilly weather—but from that time onwards the heavens were uniformly cloudless, and the least motion was weakening—nay, almost exhausting.

Hence, during this immoderate heat, the streets in La Valette are well nigh deserted from ten o'clock in the morning until four, in the afternoon. All the parades, therefore, were held after the latter hour, and care was taken to accommodate each sentinel with a shady station.

The atmosphere, meanwhile, is very pure and cheerful; and as one breathes much more freely, it is, for weak lungs, extremely favourable. The evenings are (particularly in June) so clear that Mount Etna can be seen from hence quite plainly; and when its point is yet gilded by the sun, whilst at Malta the dusk is already gathering, the prospect is beautiful in the highest degree.

Chapter 26

Disembarkation

In the beginning of the month of July, instructions were communicated for us to hold ourselves in readiness to pursue our voyage to Sicily, and on the 4th we were already embarked. Our battalion was accommodated in five Maltese vessels and one English. On the 7th instant the wind served, in the evening we got under weigh, and on the following morning passed Cape Passaro, arriving that same day close in the vicinity of Mount Etna.

A contrary wind, however, now sprang up, against which we had to contend until the 14th, with the exception of an occasional calm. Hence, we sailed extremely slow, and were consequently gratified by keeping Etna all the while in sight, whilst, on the other side, the Calabrian hills were seen absolutely lifting themselves into the skies. The little town of Catanea, at the foot of the volcano, was likewise perceptible from the deck; but on Etna itself no object could be distinguished, and it towered into the heavens one dense black mass. Its crest was surrounded by clouds, but when a transitory breeze blew these aside, its crater was developed, and appeared of immense circumference.

I did not observe any snow upon it, which, during the summer months, is confined to the crevices below. As we approached Messina the Strait grew very narrow indeed; and, in consequence, the shore of Calabria, with the enemy's batteries, &c. was plainly distinguishable, notwithstanding we were running close under that of Sicily.

On the morning of the 15th, as we were doubling the neck of land, shaped like a sickle, whereby the harbour of Messina is in some degree formed, the violent current which operates here had nearly driven us to the opposite and hostile shore; but, fortunately, a strong wind arose, which, coupled with the exertions of the seamen, brought us to our destination. We found the harbour very destitute of shipping, as an expedition to Alicant, in Spain, had just been despatched thence, and had employed all the vessels on the station excepting a few merchant-ships.

Next day the troops disembarked, the men being quartered in a convent, and the officers in private houses. As for myself, circumstances occasioned me to go outside the city, and I was about to become an inmate of a deserted monastery; I soon found, however, that this would not do by any means, and accordingly lost no time in providing myself with regular lodgings.

The view of Messina from the harbour is extremely—I may say awfully—beautiful, as the town is built in the shape of an amphitheatre, and amongst the mass of buildings exhibits many ruinous marks of the devastation of the last earthquake. It lies at the foot of a mountain, and the space included between the two horns of the half circle may extend to a league. At the left extremity is a large strong castle which commands the harbour and town, and was built during the reign of Charles the Fifth.

On the right point lies the Fort Salvador, which completely overlooks the neck of land before alluded to; and immediately above the centre of the town are situated, on the side of a high hill, two other forts, called Gonzago and, Castelazo, by which the whole fortifications are crowned; and close under them lie several monasteries and other structures of magnitude. The Marine-street, which runs along the shore, forms a very elegant object: it was in the last earthquake completely ruined, but has been since rebuilt. The houses are generally from four to six stories high.

One of the most magnificent prospects in Europe is, without doubt, that which is commanded from the Fort Gonzago, before mentioned. Everyone who for the first time sets his foot upon the large platform in front of this citadel remains several minutes struck with admiration. Before him lies the town of Messina, and beyond it the beautiful bay, three quarters of a league in circumference, with its sickle-formed neck of land, upon the extreme point of which, at the entrance of the harbour, stands a lofty light-house.

Further on, the Strait, or Faro, spreads itself in breadth a league, which however is contracted as it nears the Mediterranean, and on its narrowest part appears another lighthouse—the celebrated Torre de Faro. The mountains of Calabria, likewise, towering into the heavens, augment the majesty of the prospect, which towards evening is additionally enchanting, for then the surrounding hills throw Messina into shadow, whilst they themselves are still, with a kind of fairy splendour, illumined by the sun.

Up to the middle of August, 1812, an occurrence of interest had varied the monotony of our life at Messina, and we meanwhile endeavoured, on account of the overpowering heat, to keep ourselves as quiet as possible. The mustering of the troops in the glow of the sun often tried us severely. The non-commissioned officers and privates sought some relief from this annoyance by repeated plunges into the sea, but this refuge could not be resorted to during the night, which was frequently hotter than the day, as in the latter a slight breeze occasionally struck up, which was seldom or never the case at night-time.

At the latter end of the same month, a jubilee was celebrated by the English and Sicilian troops, in honour of the victory gained by Lord Wellington at Salamanca. The Strait, for a distance exceeding two leagues, was, in order to prevent the possibility of a landing from the opposite shore, defended by a strong force of artillery, between the different pieces whereof troops were stationed, and everything being arranged, a fire was commenced, which ran from battery to battery and from division to division, and produced a very grand and striking effect

The month of November in Sicily bears the appearance of

a fine spring or autumn season. The heat relaxes, the trees are covered with leaves, which begin to assume every variety of hue, and the fields bloom in delightful verdure.

During the preceding summer-months vegetation is checked from want of sufficient moisture, and it now takes a fresh spring and yields in abundance the culinary treasures of the garden, particularly the most delicious broccoli, white cabbage, &c. The growth of the cauliflower here is indeed surprising, its stalk commonly reaching three feet in height, its leaves spreading over a circumference of several yards, and its head large enough to dine two or three persons: but against this unusual bulk may be placed the fact that it is not equally tender with the produce of the same nature in Germany.

The pumpkin, which is also of monstrous size, frequently forms a dish for the poorer classes. Potatoes are not much cultivated here, for the soil is by no means so friendly to their produce as that of colder climates, and in consequence the vegetable is by no means so well tasted. Green peas are reared without any trouble, in the open air, throughout the months of December and January, as likewise are salads.

In fact, it is not unusual in well-kept gardens (particularly in those appertaining to monasteries) to see fresh supplies of vegetables springing up every three months, so that, in the course of a year, they often gather their crops four times. But, in speaking of the vegetable produce of Sicily, we must by no means overlook the Indian fig, which is esteemed not only a luxury but a positive necessary both by rich and poor, who even imagine, in the latter end of the summer, that the eating of this fruit is material to their health. It is, in short, almost the universal breakfast and supper, and its growth is so much encouraged that for the smallest coin one may procure above half a dozen. The trees whereon it grows are sturdy and rough, requiring little or no cultivation, and in some instances springing up so thickly as to wear the appearance of huge forests.

The prodigious number of grape-vines which adorn both the hills and valleys produce several sorts of wine, which are some of them extremely pleasant, and the principal whereof are those denominated Marsalla, Siracusa, Catania, and Faro;—these all possess a fine flavour and much fire.

But although Sicily produces so many excellent wines, there is no disposition on the part of the inhabitants to avail themselves thereof inordinately, and it is very rare indeed to encounter one of them in a state of inebriation. In fact, Mohammed's law is strictly observed here by many Christian families, who, in conformity therewith, drink no wine at all, notwithstanding it is to be had so freely. In all hot climates, the too plentiful use of wine is particularly injurious, especially to the foreigner.

Independently of the fruits and vegetables enumerated above, this island abounds in others of a description almost equally luxurious, in spite of which profusion, however, it would be well nigh impossible to meet, in any other country, (taking the relative amount of population into the estimate,) so many beggars and famished-looking wretches.

Christmas is kept here with much form and observance. For several weeks before its arrival the country people flock up to Messina, and serenade the houses of their landlords there with advent-hymns, &c.; and as the festival draws nearer, these visitors increase in a very great proportion.

At twelve o'clock on Christmas Eve commences what is called the early mass, which commencement is announced by the ringing of bells, &c. On that eve, also, is set up, in the houses of both rich and poor, the customary Christmas tree,[1] laden with presents alike for old and young.

1. In Germany, this practice is likewise universal. A large bough is set up in the principal apartment at Christmastime, and all the smaller branches thereof are hung with little presents for the different members of the household, suited in point of taste and costliness to the several parties for whom they are intended. A good deal of innocent mirth and raillery is produced by this custom, which gives rise also to a spirit of kindness and courtesy, not limited to the individuals of the family.

Chapter 27

Beau-Monde of Messina

The season of the Carnival, in February, is passed with great glee, and gives occasion to many ludicrous occurrences. Daily are men and women to be seen parading the streets in the wildest and most grotesque garbs, in which masquerading the holy priesthood do not disdain to join, but on the other hand, get up numerous processions in which the prevailing object appears to be to make themselves look as ridiculous as possible.

The crowds of boys who are let loose at this period exhibit a practical commentary on these laudable efforts of the pious fathers, and run about in parties dressed as Catholic priests and wearing masks representing sheep's heads! Other persons, likewise, with an apparent and no doubt a proper consciousness of their own deserts, scruple not to parade the streets habited as criminals and with ropes round their necks.

The enemy's troops on the opposite shore captured, during the period of my stay here, several English merchant-vessels, which had been driven by contrary winds and the stream of the Faro upon the Calabrian coast, where they were immediately fired upon with effect, in spite of the efforts to succour them made by throwing bombs from our side.

At length, on the 15th of February, an English regiment of infantry, under cover of a flotilla of gun-boats, was despatched to the opposite shore—the object in sending them being to destroy the enemy's magazine and batteries. This object was fully obtained, and we soon perceived the fire and smoke which resulted creeping along the sides of the mountains and staining the pure ether with their ghastly and stifling masses.

By way of diversion, during the accomplishment of this service, our battalion, together with others, was marched along shore to the point directly opposite Reggio, with a great deal of parade, and as conspicuously as possible, in order to attract the attention of the enemy. By daybreak this movement was commenced, and by eleven o'clock a. m. we were again in our quarters, whilst the troops which had been engaged in the actual performance of the duty returned towards evening; bringing with them several hundred prisoners. On our side, a few men only were killed and wounded.

The *beau-monde* of Messina drive, on the sultry summer evenings, along the shore of the Faro, which exhales a refreshing coolness, in really elegant equipages:—in good truth, it is said that many of these Sicilians prefer the *éclat* arising from such gaudy establishments to comforts of a more substantial nature at home. To be sure, a carriage of some sort is absolutely necessary in order to derive either benefit or pleasure from taking the air, on account of the oppressive heats—still, however, love of fashion and fondness for display are doubtless the prime stimulants to the practice.

After these excursions, the custom of the country prescribes a visit to the opera, which, in Messina, is not of first-rate attractions: the orchestra is tolerably good, and the singers just of such a nature as entitles them to be "damned with faint praise;" but the scenery is very inefficient and the house itself worse than mediocre. From the opera, the well-dressed mob adjourn to private *conversazióni,* whereat gambling is carried on to considerable extent and deep into the night.

In the cool months—namely, from November to February, the troops were constantly exercised, and frequently despatched on little expeditions into the surrounding country. At the end of the latter month, in the year 1813, the 77th English Regiment and the 7th and 8th Battalions of the German Legion, unexpectedly received orders to march away from Messina, but our destination was not communicated, since upon the secrecy of our movements depended (as it subsequently turned out) the success of a very important measure.

On the 27th, early in the morning, accordingly, we departed, taking the way to Milazzo, across the hill which borders the Faro. (Milazzo is distant from Messina about twenty-five miles.) Over this mountainous tract, the English, during their ascendancy in the island, had opened a road, which considerably eased the passage, though it still remained precipitous and difficult.

On the summit batteries have been constructed, and barracks built capable of accommodating several thousand men; and thus the passage of the Strait is effectually commanded. The existence of these fortifications, &c. is the more worthy of remark, as it must have been necessary, for the purpose of their erection, to drag up by pulleys all the building-materials, as well as the pieces of artillery, which consisted chiefly of twenty-four pounders.

Late in the afternoon of the before-mentioned day, we arrived at this same town of Milazzo, the appearance of which was anything but prepossessing; and had I not been accustomed to numerous ill-looking places in Spain and Portugal, the sight of it would have made me quite melancholy. We were lodged in the cells of monks, who, to judge from their domiciles, could not have thought it necessary to add the principle of cleanliness to that of devotion.

In the Anglo-Sicilian army, a custom had been established, by directions from head-quarters, whereby the troops, to expedite their movements, marched without baggage, which was despatched after them by water:—the few matters of indispensable utility being included in knapsacks, which were not only carried, as is universal, by the privates, but strapped to the backs of the officers also;—an arrangement which, notwithstanding its prevalence in the continental armies, has a novel character amongst English military.

Milazzo lies upon a hilly neck of land opposite the Liparian islands, two of which are eternally smoking, and often discharge volumes of flame. The principal buildings of this place are convents and monasteries. Art has been but little exercised, in the construction either of the town or the harbour; the latter of which is merely formed by the neck of land whereon the former stands.

On the morning of the 28th, several transports, together with a ship of war, ran into the harbour, and in these were embarked, towards afternoon, the three battalions. We now acquired some information relative to the service on which we were bound, and which proved to be an expedition to Palermo, to strengthen the English garrison of that capital, as some disturbance was apprehended, in consequence of certain projected measures against the Queen of Sicily,—the nature whereof was still, to us, wrapt in uncertainty.

On the 1st of March, 1813, this flotilla of twelve vessels, with their convoy, sailed from out the harbour of Milazzo. The wind was not friendly to us in starting, and by the time we had doubled Cape Marsalla, it blew still more adverse, so that we were not only obliged to cruise two days and nights about the Liparian islands, but, towards the evening of the third day, found ourselves compelled to anchor in a creek some twelve miles from Milazzo, where we remained, owing to the prevalence of contrary winds, until the 5th instant.

On the 6th we were enabled to get off, and arrived by sunset in the harbour of Palermo. This voyage, with a favourable wind, might have been accomplished in twelve hours, instead of which seven days had been thus consumed. Had the roads been easily practicable, we might, indeed, have made the distance by land in a few hours only. For single passengers, or mules, the way might be well enough, but for large bodies, or even for horses, it was incommodious, nay, dangerous; as was abundantly experienced by the horses belonging, to our battalion, which traversed it, on account of there not being room for them in the vessels.

Chapter 28

Disembarkation at the Mola

Having disembarked at Palermo, we were, as at Milazzo, quartered in a monastery, called Convento Anuntiata, in which immense edifice 3000 men, including the greater part of the officers, were comprised. Besides the forces thus introduced, there were already 900 British soldiers in the city.

Palermo, the capital of Sicily, and at that time the residence of the King of Naples, lies on a large plain, several leagues in circumference, and close to the sea. This plain is enclosed by an amphitheatre of high and barren mountains, at the foot whereof are a whole bevy of convents, together with numerous country-houses, surrounded by large gardens. The aspect of this important city, with its many towers, is extremely beautiful from the sea.

We landed at the Mola, close to the suburb of St. Lucie, where a neck of land branching from Monte Pellegrino forms a harbour, not very extensive, and difficult to clear out from; and hence our vessel had cast anchor immediately at its entrance, and we were put ashore in small boats. The extremity of this neck of land is defended by a fort, and another of considerable dimensions (the fort *à Mare)* lies just in front of the town. The Mola, as it is called, is the shore of the harbour, and is well-paved: upon it is the arsenal, and close adjoining a large prison. A number of boats, their keels uppermost, strewed the shore, and fanned miserable lurking-places for a crowd of half-naked and half-famished wanderers from the coast of Naples.

Palermo takes a very high rank amongst. European cities: it is enclosed by a lofty wall; and may be estimated to contain 200,000 inhabitants. Its extent, however, is rather in length than in breadth; its figure elliptical, and it has, without-side the walls, several suburbs. The two principal streets, which intersect the town at right angles, are each of them nearly half a league in length. They are quite, straight: the longest, *Strada del Casaro,* (or *di Toledo,)* takes its commencement from the sea-shore, with a high gate, called *Porta Felice,* and terminates in the vicinity of the royal palace, with a still more lofty and splendid gate—*Porta Nuova;* and beyond it runs, for the space of a league, in the same line, the beautiful road to Montreal.

All the, houses throughout this extensive and elegant street rise, from five to seven stories in height, and among them are many palaces of the nobility. The ground-floor of these palaces, however, is generally appropriated to shopkeepers, whilst above, the most elegant balconies protrude themselves, whereon are to be frequently seen promenading, the families of the aristocratic owners of the structure.

The other principal street, the *Strada Nuova,* (or *di Marqueda,)* is not quite so distinguished, but is still beautiful; and its houses intermixed with palaces, churches, and monasteries. From the point whereat these two streets cross each other, the eye of the spectator commands the four chief gates of the city. The pavements are constituted of broad pieces of lava. Underneath the houses there are, also, shops, or stalls, whereat all sorts, of fancy-goods, together with articles of provision, are vended, as in a sort of bazaar, and these kind of places are likewise particular appropriated as workshops for artisans.

But with the *Strada del Casaro* and the *Strada Nuova* all the beauty of Palermo terminates—so far, at least, as regards the buildings of the town; for the other streets are narrow, dark, and filthy; and, in the evening, their perambulation is extremely dangerous, especially to strangers, who are frequently waylaid and robbed, and often assassinated. The squares are far too small to accommodate the mass of buyers and sellers, wherewith they are constantly filled, and who flock in fairly by crowds; there are, however, two exceptions, the King's and the Marine Squares.

I have already, in a former part of these *memorandums*, observed upon the singular blending, in the metropolis of Ireland, of opulence and poverty—of luxury and destitution: the same remark will hold good with respect to the metropolis of Sicily, and to a still greater degree. Before the palace of the proud noble are frequently seen a number of wretched-looking objects, whose misery contrasts strangely with the gaudy equipage and liveried host of their lordly fellow-citizen. They are suffered to lie unnoticed and famishing, nor does their forlorn condition apparently excite the least commiseration in the bosoms of the favourites of Fortune.

The coaches of the Sicilian nobility are chiefly constructed in London, and transported thither at immense cost. This kind of expenditure is by no means grudgingly applied; but were a fellow-creature literally perishing for want at his threshold, I doubt if a *grandee* of Palermo would sanction the slightest outgoing to rescue him from his impending fate.

The plain surrounding the city is laid out in gardens, which contain abundance of delicious fruit The soil is extremely productive, and capable of yielding nourishment to an immense number of people; and, did not the spirit of indolence prevail, there need be little or no privation felt by the natives of the island. It is true, this produce is in a great measure monopolized by the troops of lazy monks, which throng about in all directions; for these worthies, with that tact wherewith they are seldom unprovided, have pitched their residences upon the most fruitful spots in the neighbourhood.

Monks, in fact, and beggars, are, if I may so express myself, the staple nuisances of Palermo; and an English officer would not be long in discovering the annoyance of the latter, as they beset him on all sides, and he finds himself compelled, in order to fight his way through, to distribute some trifling gratuities, for which act of kindness he is generally repaid by attempts upon his watch or purse; for a Sicilian beggar is uniformly a thief;—he is dexterous at his trade, too, as I myself had more than once the misfortune to discover.

A British officer, on one occasion, gave a female beggar a Spanish dollar: close by stood a mendicant friar, who, the moment after, stepped up with his poor-box, and showed her a representation upon its lid of the flames of hell; whereupon the terrified creature flung the alms she had just received into the treasury of the knavish priest. The officer, however, having witnessed this transaction, immediately made up to the friar, and by dint of a good deal of entreaty, and a few threats, compelled him to refund. The woman imagined that she should get the dollar again; but the officer, by this time grown wiser, confided it to a securer place—his own pocket.

But if there is little done in Palermo towards bettering the condition of the poor while alive, a great deal of trouble is taken about their souls; and every week men are sent round to solicit the contributions of the charitable, for the purpose of purchasing masses, to pray the spirits of the dead out of purgatory!

In the middle of the month of March, I had an opportunity of witnessing the effects of an eruption of Mount Etna. For several days the atmosphere was completely obscured, not, however, with masses of cloud, but with dense wreaths of smoke. In the direction of the volcano, (which, in clear weather, can be distinctly seen from Palermo, although at the distance of a hundred miles,) the horizon wore a hue of fiery red; and, on the succeeding Sunday, there was a shower of ashes, which lasted several hours, but was followed by the clearing up of the atmosphere, and the return of fair weather.

At the conclusion of the same month, the political measures to which I formerly alluded were, at length, made known and put into execution. The queen, it appeared, had for a considerable time carried on a secret correspondence with the enemy, dangerous, at once, to her own interests and to those of the ally of Sicily: nor was the intrigue confined to herself—several of the nobility had participated therein, and, on its discovery, had been either executed or banished. They had formed a plan to surprise and disarm the English soldiers in Sicily; and, on account of this, and other circumstances which were not divulged, it was resolved to compel the queen to leave the country. She, however, feeling, as may be imagined, much chagrin at this resolution, put every possible stratagem in play to elude it.

Chapter 29

Marching Orders

Such was the state of things when, on the 24th of March, a corps, consisting of 3000 men, received orders to march from Palermo to the vicinity of Castel Veterano, a country-seat of the queen, (where at that period she was residing,) in order to superintend her departure, and preserve tranquillity. The king, who had long since abandoned the reins of government to his son, the Crown Prince, and was stopping at a royal villa near the metropolis, was equally adverse to the measures contemplated against his consort, although, as subsequently appeared, his interest was forwarded thereby; and Lord Bentinck, the British commander, received intelligence that some scheme was in agitation, whereby the misguided monarch hoped to frustrate the measures undertaken by his British allies in furtherance of the common cause.

This scheme was no sooner communicated to his Lordship, than he took effectual means to counteract it. Every morning, the whole of the garrison, amounting to 15,000 men, were turned out at daybreak, and kept under arms till noon; and on the day of the king's arrival in the capital, (which was fixed for carrying into execution this royal plot,) Lord Bentinck, in a personal interview, expressed to His Majesty his determination to halt at no measure which might appear necessary to preserve peace.

This intimation had the desired effect; yet, notwithstanding, the day did not pass over without some disturbance: and the crowd evinced dispositions to riot, under the stale plea of the scarcity of bread occasioned by the presence of the British troops. A few bullets, however, from the English patrols, soon overcame these manifestations of an evil spirit, and quiet was for awhile restored.

There were not wanting those, nevertheless, who spoke of the probability of a second Sicilian Vespers; nor were other threats of a similar nature spared. As our troops, however, were not quartered singly upon the citizens, but lay together by thousands in large monasteries; and as the Sicilian military stood firmly on our side—at least, the greater portion—we should have been enabled to repel any attack. A few stray officers and privates were ill-treated in the streets towards nightfall, being pelted with stones, and in some instances assailed with greater violence on which occasions, the guard issued from the different convents, and fired amongst the assailants through the narrow streets.

On the 25th inst. I marched with the beforementioned corps; namely, one English and two German battalions of infantry, two companies of English light dragoons, and four small pieces of artillery, (the whole under the command of General Von Hinnüber,) from Palermo to the queen's country residence. The artillery and its appurtenances was, owing to the irregularity of the mountainous roads, conveyed upon mules. At the commencement of our march we traversed a fine highway, for the space of about ten miles, over the plain of Palermo. We then began to ascend the side of the hill, proceeding several miles along a serpentine track, while masses of rock threatened us overhead and deep chasms yawned beside our feet.

Towards evening we reached the town of Piana del Greci, a small place and insufficient to lodge our whole force, the greater part of which were consequently necessitated to bivouac in an abominably damp meadow. Next morning we broke up early and pursued our route, which at length led us to Corleone, where we remained three days, to allow the queen time to form her determination and make her arrangements. Piquets, however, in addition to the usual sentinels, were carefully stationed, to guard against any surprise; and a third part of the forces were held in readiness, both day and night, in case of attack from the queen's party.

On the 29th instant, we advanced about twelve miles further, to Contessa, and the following day some ten miles more, to Santa Margaritta: although these distances were short, still, in consequence of the precipitous nature of the ground and the atrocious state of the roads, their accomplishment overwhelmed us with fatigue, and it was with no little satisfaction we found our quarters at the last-mentioned place extremely agreeable, as they were established in a commodious monastery, a large granary, and a royal palace!

As some time was expended before all the necessary arrangements could be made for our ultimate proceedings, the troops took advantage of the interval to indulge themselves with pretty free libations of the excellent wine which is here produced, and which, owing to the small communication with other districts, was vended uncommonly cheap.

On the morning of the 30th, the English regiment, the 77th, proceeded alone to a spot still nearer the residence of the Sicilian Queen, whilst the rest of the troops remained at Santa Margaritta. On the third day of our stay at this place, an officer, Captain Von Waldhausen, of the 8th Battalion, was reported missing. He had the previous day requested leave of absence, in order to take an excursion of some few miles, for the purpose of making observations and sketches of certain picturesque ruins. His prolonged absence could not but render his comrades suspicious of evil; and, accordingly, a party was detached in search of him, by which he was discovered in a defile of the mountains inhumanly murdered.

It afterwards appeared that, while sitting upon a rock, his attention busily occupied, he had been surprised by two armed Sicilians, and shot dead by repeated discharges, after which he had been despoiled of all the gold lace adorning his uniform, of his money, his watch, and other valuables. Information of this act of atrocity having been forwarded to the commander-in-chief at Palermo, his Lordship directed all proper measures to be taken to discover the culprits—threatening the inhabitants of that district with the severest penalties unless they delivered the offenders into his hands. This had the effect of detecting one of the ruffians, who, being sent to the metropolis, was punished by the loss first of his right hand and then of his head. The other accomplished his escape.

The few days which we had been told it might be necessary for us to abide in this region, in order to bring the Queen of Sicily to reason, were in the long run magnified into as many months—as that princess pleaded, in the first instance, the untimely season, and in the second, want of money, as preventives to her departure. These two pleas, however, having been put aside by time and circumstances, ill-health was next advanced in way of excuse; but this ground was likewise overruled by the decision of Dr. Calvert, so that at length, (at the beginning of June,) Her Majesty found it inevitable to embark on board a Sicilian frigate, wherein she was conveyed (under the protection of a British line-of-battle ship) to Constantinople, and thence, as is well known, travelled overland to Vienna. These vessels had been lying for upwards of two months in a small creek near the point of her residence.

During our tedious stay in these parts, I once obtained a leave of absence, enabling me to visit Palermo, which, by following a short cut across the mountains, I reached in one day. It was incumbent on me, however, to return speedily, and I had no further opportunity of eluding the intolerable dullness of our residence at Santa Margaritta, whence, to the unspeakable joy of all parties, we broke up en the 17th of May, 1813, at midnight, and arrived, next morning at nine, at Corleone.

In order to avoid, this time, lodging with the monies, I looked out for a tavern, but could find none that was at all desirable; for travellers here, as in Spain, make it a rule to carry their provisions with them; and consequently, in these inns there is nothing to be met with but chocolate, wine, and water. On the present occasion I wanted neither of the former, but was compelled to pay as much as if I had taken both. Even in Palermo itself there is only one decent inn to be found, and that is kept by an Englishwoman.

On the 20th, the troops once more reached the capital, and tranquillity was but slightly disturbed during our stay, in spite of the measures which had been deemed necessary. Some anxiety was indeed felt in anticipation of the approaching Rosalia festival, and many reports tended to excite alarm. A few days after my return to Palermo a circumstance occurred which abundantly proves how common the practice of wearing stilettos is in that town.

On changing a lodging which I had occupied outside the city, I despatched two privates of the battalion upon certain commissions; after they had executed these, the men adjourned to an adjoining cabaret, where, owing to their ignorance of the language, they got into dispute with a Sicilian.

While this dispute was going on, I arrived near the spot, and found half a dozen fellows, with daggers in their hands, following each of my men, who, already bleeding fast, were hurrying towards the nearest guard. I hastened my pace, and the first person whom I encountered was a priest, very complacently surveying the affair! Annoyed at the nonchalance of this man, I reproached him bitterly therewith, and having at length succeeded in stimulating him, he interposed and addressed a few words to his countrymen, which had the result of quieting them immediately.

Scarce a week passed, in fact, without some of our troops being poniarded; and if vengeance were not taken by ourselves, it was in vain to look for it elsewhere, as the assassins had no difficulty in finding shelter with their priests.

Thus, about a twelve-month previously, a servant of Lord Stewart, then English commander-in-chief, was murdered in the open street. The guard, without loss of time, pursued the assassin, but he obtained sanctuary in a monastery, the door of which was instantly locked. Lord Stewart demanded the surrender of the culprit, but without effect, and he found it necessary to advance against the place with a company of English grenadiers, whereupon the gates were opened, and the criminal discovered concealed behind the altar.—Upon the arrival of our troops a prohibition had been issued against the wearing of daggers, and the men had received directions to arrest every individual upon whom they found such an instrument. The regulation was, nevertheless, eluded, and stabbing remorselessly carried on.

The degree of power arrogated by the priests over the mass of the community is illustrated by the following instance:—it was no uncommon sight to observe groups of idlers lying about upon the ground engaged in gambling. On passing such a group, an ecclesiastic would go up and in a peremptory tone require the delivery of the cards. With much humility, these were uniformly rendered, and the gamblers, kissing the hand of the priest, would meekly entreat absolution, whilst he coolly pocketed the cards and walked away!

As on the days of the patron-saints everything was combined to give solemnity to their celebration, the prior had in various instances solicited of the colonel the use of our military band; so much had our stay here tended to liberalize the notions of the Catholic clergy, who, ten years before, would have deemed it sacrilege to enlist any portion of a heretic soldiery into the celebration of their festivals.

The feast of St. Rosalia now approached: but instead of awaiting the anniversary, the anticipated disturbances exploded several days before—whether intentionally or prematurely I cannot pretend to determine. Certain, however, it is, that in the latter days of June the mob accumulated, and raised cries of "Down with the English constitution! We have no bread! Down with the Parliament!"[1]

At the same time, a desperate assault was made upon the public prison, with a view to the liberation of those confined therein, but the ardour of the assailants was checked by virtue of sundry pieces of artillery being drawn up in front of that edifice.

1. A parliament had been summoned under the protection of the English General, and the Crown-Prince proclaimed Regent.

Several bakers' shops, however, were broken into and plundered, and many individuals seriously hurt Some of the mutineers were afterwards executed, and their heads placed over the arches of the city gates—a barbarous practice, gradually becoming obsolete amongst civilized states, and now almost confined to the savages of Constantinople.

It may be as well here to remark that, so far from being burdensome, the residence of the English troops was actually beneficial to this metropolis—inasmuch as they brought money into circulation. Every citizen who could spare any portion of his dwelling had been called on to state the same to the quarter-master-general, whereupon some of the staff, or other officers, were lodged there, which accommodation was liberally remunerated:—even the monasteries wherein the British forces were quartered received corresponding pay. Add to this the various subsidies, and the cash spent by the soldiers in different articles either of utility or luxury, and the result must necessarily appear favourable to the inhabitants. Besides, the very object of our being there was to keep off the French, who, as is well known, uniformly lived at free quarters in the countries they invaded.

Chapter 30

Eruption of Mount Etna

The festival of Rosalia (the patron-saint of Palermo) extends from the 7th to the 14th of July. According to the legend, her saintship had earned this distinction on account of her meritorious conduct during a period of pestilence; and on the present year it was thought advisable to celebrate the festival with peculiar solemnity, as symptoms of plague were understood to have exhibited themselves on the adjacent island of Malta.

For several previous weeks various preparations had been making in different parts of the city, and at two o'clock in the afternoon of the 7th the ceremonies commenced. A recapitulation of these would be very tiresome to the reader; we shall therefore content ourselves with stating that the triumphal car whereon the image of the saint appeared in all her glory was exceedingly rich, the crowd exceedingly devout, and the Protestant spectators exceedingly *ennuyés*. There was an illumination of three nights, wherein, among other shows, Mount Etna was burned in effigy; and, what was still better than all this, the festival went off without the least symptom of insurrection.

In the neighbourhood of my residence at Palermo stands an Augustine monastery, wherein upwards of ten thousand bodies have been kept in a state of preservation in a subterranean vault. They stand in rows, as if living; and the name is attached to each. The connexions of the, deceased are admitted at anytime, but the anniversary of St. Augustine is the favourite period for visiting, this, receptacle, and for a fortnight previous: whole crowds of people—including rich and poor—high-born and low—old and young—throng thither, counting their beads as they go, in order to, pray for the repose of the dead; but on the Saint's day itself every avenue to the monastery is blocked up with candidates for admission, and in the evening high mass is celebrated, whilst the whole of, the church, the monastery, and the vault is brilliantly illuminated.

In the spring of 1814, great preparations were made for the reconquering of Naples; these had the beneficial result of drawing off the attention of the disaffected; and, consequently, all the English forces (with the exception of our battalion and some few other troops) were employed on an expedition to the Neapolitan capital. When all was ready for embarkation, a fire broke out on board one of the transports, which occasioned a great deal of damage and delayed the proceeding.

Some months after the capture of Naples had been effected; the king set sail in order once more to take possession of his continental dominions. It was a beautiful afternoon when two English line-of-battle ships and a frigate, all their sails set, lay-to before the shore. At three o'clock, His Majesty arrived at the Marine Square, where he entered a boat and proceeded to the ships under, a royal salute. This interesting spectacle called to the minds of myself and my comrades our separation from our native land, and encouraged in us hopes that we also should, ere long, be enabled to greet it once more.

The character of, the Sicilians is strongly tinctured with choleric and revengeful feelings, and the expressive nature of their language is well calculated to manifest such emotions, even the most accomplished of the natives hesitate not to vent their anger or spleen in violent terms in the public streets. At the same time they are extremely fond of coming upon their foe from ambuscade—a method of warfare more convenient then honourable.

The following incident may serve as a proof of their attachment to open hostility An officer of the Brunswick Hussars had been publicly insulted by a police-agent, who had been compelled to make as public an apology; some reservation, however, appearing in this, the former resolved to challenge his assailant, which coming to the ears of the latter, he ensconced himself cautiously in his house, which he got filled with armed men, and at length contrived to abstract himself altogether from the town.

The Sicilians are not a very hospitable people. Several of our officers who had learnt to speak the language fluently, and flattered themselves that they might consequently stand a chance of gaining admission into families, found little or no encouragement given to their advances.

In the spring of the following year, 1815, all the British troops, with the exception of our battalion, were despatched to Genoa, in order to capture and occupy that city, thus leaving Palermo almost wholly destitute of the red coats, who had for so long a period held the upper hand there. The few soldiers remaining behind were scarcely sufficient to keep watch over the treasury and arsenals of the army.

I was very desirous, during my stay upon this island, to have an opportunity of visiting Mount Etna whilst in a state of eruption, but in that wish I was not indulged. The following account is from the pen of a friend; and as the phenomena it describes are amongst the most interesting scenes of Sicily, I trust no apology will be necessary for introducing it.

Account of Two Visits to Mount Etna, Whilst in a State of Eruption.

We were quartered in Syracuse, and were sitting at table, at six o'clock in the evening, when some person burst into our apartment, and, in a hurried manner, informed us that Etna was completely enveloped in flames. The company immediately rose abruptly, and rushed out to witness the sublime spectacle. We stood gazing thereat for some time,—the fiery stream flowing in three separate divisions, and the sky above our heads appearing blood-red.

On the following morning, a party, of officers, (including myself) engaged a boat and sailed to Catania, where we arrived at, three o'clock in the afternoon. Guides and mules were forthwith procured; and having furnished ourselves with provisions, we commenced our journey to the fire at seven o'clock, p. m. The distance from Catania to the point of the eruption, was about eighteen or twenty miles, and the night as warm, as any in the month of July, in Germany.

The moon gave a bright and steady lustre; and by two next morning we reached Soffrano, a village lying in a woody region, between seven and eight miles from the spot we were travelling to. Already, at Catania, we had plainly distinguished the crackling, and rushing of the fire, and as we approached more nearly to the agitated mountain the roaring; noise increased, until, at length, it resembled thunder, and exceeded the report from a battery of a hundred cannon.

As we journeyed, on, in awe-stricken silence, suddenly the bright moon dipped her horns beneath a rolling mass of smoke, and the glare of the flaming volcano became more frightful and unearthly. The only road from Soffrano up the mountain was that which had been beaten out by the goatherds and their charges: it was rugged, precipitous, and unsure, being strewed with loose stones and pieces of lava, which slipped from underneath the feet and occasioned several of my companions to stumble, though none of them, fortunately, received material injury.

Besides these obstructions, the fierce flames, which occasionally burst forth with renewed fury, fairly blinded us, whilst the palpable darkness wherein these eager emissaries were absorbed, and, which wrapt every other quarter of the heavens, was startling from the powerful contrast, and between the one and the other; we were utterly unable to see any surrounding object; Under these circumstances, the guides, parties of whom both preceded and followed us, shouted to each other, in order to keep the company from separation, which; nevertheless, in spite of their endeavours, did actually take place. We met again, however, at the extreme point of ascent, which we arrived at, after great exertion, about four o'clock, a. m.

From the spot which we had now reached, this grand phenomenon of nature was displayed in all its gloomy majesty before us. We paused, spellbound with admiration and wonder. The spectacle was truly splendid, and it was said, that no eruption equally powerful had occurred for a considerable length of time.

One of the craters lay far above our heads in the cold region; and as it was impossible to distinguish the contour of the mountain, the stream which flowed from the aperture appeared as if fantastically spouting from out of the heavens themselves: the principle seat of the eruption was much lower.

There is a rock here shaped like a tower, and consequently denominated *Il Torre di Mazaro* on both sides of this rock; the angry mountain vomited its boiling masses with incredible violence—a fiery fountain playing, as it were, around the flinty bosom of the *Torre*. From one of these openings, stones of a hundred weight flew out, and fell again with stunning reverberation: but the tower remained immoveable—as if absolutely defying the principle of destruction.

Our present distance from the actual seat of eruption might have been some thousand steps, and hence we could plainly distinguish the alteration in the aspect of the lava, which, on its first discharge, glows like liquid fire, but as it recedes from the crater becomes gradually black. It dashes onwards (although rather slowly) with irresistible force—making way over every object which it cannot displace.

If a tree is encountered by the stream, it is in flames immediately; and the earth around literally trembles, as if struck with fear at the portentous agitation of her entrails. With caution, however, we found ourselves enabled to advance almost close to the lava-current, and in fact some of our company had sufficient temerity to light their *meerschaums* thereat:—this turned out, it is true, to have been rather hazardous, than wise, as they experienced inconvenience from the effluvia of the brimstone.

At dawn of day, the splendour of the scene waxed dim, and the flames, like shuddering ghosts, crept back again into the recesses of the volcano; we therefore deemed it no longer interesting to remain; and feeling a very considerable aspiration after breakfast, made as rapid a descent as possible.

Catania is, without exception, one of the most beautiful towns in Europe. The streets are quite straight, and several of them lined with absolute palaces, whilst the trading part of the place exhibits greater marks of opulence than any other town of Sicily—Palermo excepted. It contains a university, together with several silk-manufactories; and possesses the privilege of exemption from any military governor or garrison.

Lying so near to Mount Etna, it has often been visited by shocks of earthquake, and at one or two epochs completely upset; but has still arisen from its ashes with fresh beauty. The year 1665 and 1688 were particularly ruinous to Catania, and sundry palaces still remain in an imperfect state.

I visited the crater of Etna at another point of time. As the inns in Sicily are not duly detestable, but at the same time rarely to be met with even such as they are, it is indispensable, in travelling, to carry every requisite with one,—the road from Messina runs, for the most part, along the sea. The first place of any importance on the route is Salietta, belonging to a prince of that name.

We next arrive at Torriena, (formerly Naxos,) which exhibits an extraordinary instance of the caprices of destiny; it is said to have once possessed 100,000 Greek inhabitants, but is now reduced to a more wretched assemblage of huts, nor does anything exist to indicate its former *grandeur* except some well-preserved ruins of an ancient theatre: this town was demolished by the Saracens in the year 1280.

On ascending higher, the traveller reaches the monastery Nicolosi, and about a quarter of a league beyond this, a lava-field presents itself, which assumes at first sight the aspect of a sea with all its waves, fixed, as if by the rod of a magician, whilst in the very season of agitation. Next, he advances to a forest belonging to the Prince of Palermo.

I and my companions had already found it necessary to put on our great coats—so different did the atmosphere become on our ascent into the higher region: but now the cold was so intense, that we found it requisite to betake ourselves to our mantles likewise, whilst one of our mule-drivers, a young lad of twelve years of age, fell upon the earth, completely benumbed. Thus did we continue gradually to ascend, I may say, almost without metaphor, to the very sky; and the features of the scene grew quite savage, and withal so gloomy, that we could scarce see five steps beyond us.

At a distance of about five miles from the crater, stands a small house; this we reached after nightfall; and here it appeared as though we stood upon an island—whilst underneath our feet huge masses of cloud rolled and heaved like the restless waves of ocean, and overhead, the moon and stars once more sailed majestically, having escaped from their vapoury concealment. Meantime silence profound, primeval, deathlike, contributed to invest every surrounding object with additional solemnity, and to impress our minds with a feeling that we were separated from all other living beings.

We had not stood upon this spot above five minutes, when the crater resumed its angry operations by throwing up vast masses of stone, each explosion bursting on the ear like an award of fate, and scattering the silence as the uprising sun dispels the darkness of night. About four o'clock, a. m. the clouds which had filled the air both below and around us began to dissipate, and we resumed our progress to the very point of the crater afoot, being obliged to spring from one firm spot to another.

Underneath the crater, are several small fissures: into one of these I plunged my stick, and on drawing it out again, found it completely covered with brimstone. We had now to proceed along a road formed of ashes, which stratum we understood to be uncommonly deep; a kind of path exceedingly irksome to the traveller.

The sun, as we attained the summit of our adventurous expedition, was just in the act of lifting his broad disk over the horizon, and it would require an abler pen than mine to paint in its true colours the enchanting scene which its rays developed. The whole kingdom of Sicily lay before us spread out like a map: besides which, the eye commanded the region of Calabria, the island of Malta, the Liparian and even the Ionian islands!—The crater itself is about four miles in circumference; and when the wind is not contrary, it may be entered a little way. The blocks of stone which are emitted fly up to a great height and fall again slantingly.

Chapter 31

Conclusion

At the end of June, 1815, after a residence of three years in the island of Sicily, we likewise received instructions to embark for Genoa, and on 11th of July set sail from Palermo. As we were unattended by any convoy, and it was not deemed expedient to attempt the entire voyage without one, particularly as several large cruisers had been, fitted out from the island of Elba and had captured sundry English vessels, it was decided that we should first proceed to Naples, when we arrived after an agreeable passage (though rather long for the distance) of five days.

It was a lovely summer morning when we ran in between the isle of Capri and the mainland. The Bay of Naples is universally recognised as one of the most beautiful in the known world, and no one can fail to be much struck with its first sight. As we entered, somewhat towards the left lay exposed to view the superb city, with its numerous towers and palaces. To the right, just at the foot of Mount Vesuvius, (which formed, itself, an object of extreme grandeur and interest,) lay the town of Portici; though, from on board, that town and the capital appeared as if massed together. In the background rises the ever smoking mountain, uplifting its awful head into the clouds.

We anchored next morning near the lighthouse. At the entrance of the proper harbour of Naples. I lost no time in going ashore (accompanied by a friend who was acquainted with the place) in order to avail myself of the period of our stay, which was extremely uncertain. Here, as elsewhere, the first movements after stepping ashore are impeded by a swarm of fellows who crowd about proffering their services, though these certainly were neither so wretched-looking nor so importunate as I found their caste in Lisbon.

Among those peculiarities of the place that at once attracted my notice, were the carriages in use, which might either be driven by a coachman or by the party himself who hires one of them. In the latter case, the coachman runs alongside, whence it may be inferred that there is little capacity for speed. Of the famous *lazzaroni,* I saw few if any, as they had been, carefully incorporated by Murat in the ranks, of his army. On the Sunday, the streets here seemed to be quiet enough; but on every other day of the week it is really difficult to penetrate through the principle thoroughfares on account of the multiplicity of people who throng them.

The opera-house of San Carlos exceeded, rather than fell under, all my expectations. The orchestra was superb, and its effect singular, in as much as (from the skilful construction of the edifice) the music sounded as strong as though the house had been empty although it was literally crowded.

The museum had been greatly enlarged by the care and attention of King Joachim, and enriched with a variety of antiquities which had been exhumated at Herculaneum and Pompeii. To these ancient towns I did not neglect to pay a visit as likewise to Portici. The road thither is lined with beautiful villas. On the right the harbour is stretched out, generally filled with shipping; on the left towers the gigantic volcano. At Portici we went over the royal palace, the splendid apartments whereof contained precisely as left by Murat.

Contrary to expectation, we remained six days at anchor in the bay of Naples, and at the completion of that term set sail for Genoa, which we reached in ten days more. Having undergone quarantine, as usual, we were permitted to go ashore on the 13th of August. The aspect of the city and its bay is not a great deal inferior to that of Naples.

The bay of Genoa is smaller, but the harbour larger than that of the former metropolis, and the town lies more amphitheatrically. Before the walls of the place the largest ships of the line may, owing to the depth of the water, safely, ride at anchor.

The houses in the best parts of Genoa have their exteriors painted in a style really quite artistical, and it would scarce require much stress of fancy to imagine oneself walking in picture-gallery instead of the open street.

Many of the streets, on the other hand, are so narrow that no carriage can pass through them, and so gloomy that it is necessary to burn candles at midday. During my stay in the place, the King of Sardinia entered and took possession of it; the queen, likewise made her *entré*, and the event was celebrated with boat-racing in the bay, illuminations, and other testimonies of rejoicing. The Genoese were heartily tired of French domination; and even whilst the latter were master of the city and the English only lying before it, Bonaparte was burnt in effigy.

During my sojourn at Genoa, I visited an admirable asylum for the deaf and dumb, wherein were eighteen youths, whose education had been advanced to a most extraordinary pitch, considering their natural disqualifications. One of them was particularly accomplished, being able to read and write French, Italian, Latin, and Greek.

About the beginning of December, 1815, reports were spread that our stay would not be of much longer duration in Genoa; as, owing to the conclusion of a general peace, a considerable reduction of the British army was likely to take place, in which of course the German Legion would participate; and thus the opportunity so anxiously desired, and for awhile so little expected, be afforded us, of returning to our beloved country.

This information was indeed not quite so welcome as it would otherwise have been, on account of the dreary season of the year, and the injurious effects which a sudden removal from the burning south to a severe northern climate was calculated to produce upon our health. We should nevertheless have started in the middle of December, (according to the orders which were communicated to us,) had not the conduct of the Sardinian government occasioned our sojourn to be protracted, and we thus approached the more favourable season.

It had been stipulated between the British and Sardinian governments, that the latter was to take the horses of the Brunswick Hussars, as also the train of artillery belonging to the German Legion; at a certain valuation. This treaty, however, was disregarded; and it therefore became necessary to obtain fresh instructions from England, the tenor of which directed the horses to be put up for public sale. All this occupied time, and the spring gradually came round. Meanwhile the necessary transports were provided, by the care of General Macfarlane.

On the 11th of February, 1816, we embarked, and, forming a fleet of eight transports, ran out of the harbour of Genoa, with a heavy north-west wind, which was indeed so violent as to require all the caution of the sailors to avoid striking against one of the towers at the month of the harbour. Driven by this boisterous, though favourable, breeze, we arrived at midnight in the Gulf of Lyons, in which tempestuous anchorage we rid out a gale, and continued the space of three days.

We then proceeded to Gibraltar, where we remained two days longer, and when on the point of sailing our captain received orders to suspend operations, as the governor was desirous of increasing our company by the addition of a beautiful leopard, sent as a present to the Prince Regent. Our new messmate being safely stowed on board in an immense cage, the signal was made, and with a favourable wind we emerged from the Strait and entered the Atlantic.

After a stormy passage, we anchored near the Mother Bank, by Spithead; and having, after quarantine, sailed towards land, I once more, and for the last time, set my foot on English ground-though but for a short period, as it had been arranged that we should re-embark for Germany on the first fair wind. Consequently, I had barely time to look at the storehouses, arsenal, &c. and was quite unable to visit the metropolis, which I would fain have done, if possible.

Our departure was, indeed, abrupt; for I was awakened in the middle of the night, by an intimation that the wished-for breeze had suddenly sprung, up, and that my presence on board was requisite forthwith. By nine o'clock a. m. we weighed anchor, and with a south-west wind quitted the shore of Albion, and entered the mouth of the Ems. The quarantine laws were now again put into force, quite unnecessarily, and to our inconceivable nuisance, thus lying in sight of our beloved country, and yet not daring to spring ashore.

At length, the wished-for moment arrived. We put off in boats from the ship, and, after an absence of twelve years, I once again greeted the soil of Germany. The battalion whereto I was attached, was now, with another (the 6th), which had accompanied us from Genoa, dispersed, and I set off, full of hope and joy, for my native town.